PREPARING FOR THE
RAIN ON IWO JIMA ISLE

THE TRUE STORY OF
THE BATTLE OF IWO JIMA SURVIVOR,
MARION FRANK WALKER,
CORPORAL,
UNITED STATES
MARINE CORPS
#906419

AUTH~~ORED BY MARION FRANK WA~~LKER
AND ~~CO-AUTHORED BY~~ ~~WH~~ITE

AuthorHouse™
1663 Liberty Drive
Bloomington, IN 47403
www.authorhouse.com
Phone: 1-800-839-8640

First published by AuthorHouse 10/19/2009

ISBN: 978-1-4490-2960-9 (e)
ISBN: 978-1-4490-2958-6 (sc)
ISBN: 978-1-4490-2959-3 (hc)

Library of Congress Control Number: 2009910610

Printed in the United States of America
Bloomington, Indiana

This book is printed on acid-free paper.

Frank Walker with his wife Jackie, taken at the Marine Corps' Ball at Hyatt Regency in Indianapolis in 2007. Frank was the speaker at this event.

CONTENTS

INTRODUCTION

In opening this book, you may discover a little bit of me in yourself. Our similarities may vary, depending on who you are and your own experiences in life. You may not always agree with me, but that's okay. In fact, I fought for your right to disagree, and many of my friends gave their lives to assure that you have the right to disagree with me. We are who we are.

It is my belief that we are in great part a product of the early training (or lack thereof) in our formative years. The title of this book is apropos to my life; namely, "Preparing for the Rain on Iwo Jima Isle." If it were not for the hard times, as well as the good times during the Depression years for me and my family, I would never have understood life in the Marine Corps and the sanctity of life. It was in those formative years that I learned honor, courage, loyalty and commitment. Those values have become the substance of my life for these 84 years. Since God did not make us perfect in nature, I have slipped a little sometimes, but have always come back to what I know to be right.

It is my hope that as you read this book you will discover there is more to life than a "trip to the mall."

Rather, it should be a life given to HONOR – honoring those who through our 233 years as a country gave their lives to create the America that we know and love.

It should be a life given to LOYALTY – staying loyal to those around you if you believe they are right.

It should be a life given to COURAGE – being unafraid to stand up against society when you feel they are wrong.

And finally, COMMITMENT – staying the course, even though there might be those around you who are losing their way.

IF

By Rudyard Kipling

IF you can keep your head when all about you
Are losing theirs and blaming it on you,
If you can trust yourself when all men doubt you,
But make allowance for their doubting too;
If you can wait and not be tired by waiting,
Or being lied about, don't deal in lies,
Or being hated, don't give way to hating,
And yet don't look too good, nor talk too wise:

If you can dream - and not make dreams your master;
If you can think - and not make thoughts your aim;
If you can meet with Triumph and Disaster
And treat those two impostors just the same;
If you can bear to hear the truth you've spoken
Twisted by knaves to make a trap for fools,
Or watch the things you gave your life to, broken,
And stoop and build 'em up with worn-out tools:

If you can make one heap of all your winnings
And risk it on one turn of pitch-and-toss,
And lose, and start again at your beginnings
And never breathe a word about your loss;
If you can force your heart and nerve and sinew
To serve your turn long after they are gone,
And so hold on when there is nothing in you
Except the Will which says to them: 'Hold on!'

If you can talk with crowds and keep your virtue,
' Or walk with Kings - nor lose the common touch,
if neither foes nor loving friends can hurt you,
If all men count with you, but none too much;
If you can fill the unforgiving minute
With sixty seconds' worth of distance run,
Yours is the Earth and everything that's in it,
And - which is more - you'll be a Man, my son!

This is the Marine Corps' way as I know it. It has been this way since its inception on November 10, 1775.

As you read this book, some of the events may seem inconceivable to you, but it is a chronicle of my life which I wish to record before I leave this earth. Upon God's decision for Him to take me with Him, I can leave this earth truthfully saying that I am proud to be an American and a U.S. Marine.

Nathan Hale, an American soldier and Revolutionary officer who attempted to spy on the British was quoted to have said before he was hanged, "I only regret that I have but one life to give for my country." He was 21 years old. I would echo Mr. Hale's sentiments.

And now, I will attempt to recreate my experiences leading up to and surviving the worst battle in the history of the Marine Corps; an experience which has been one I can never forget and one that I will relive every day of my remaining years. And always remember that I am in no way a hero. According to estimates I have read, the United States losses at Iwo Jima were 6,821 killed, 19,217 wounded, and battle fatigue causalities totaled 2,648. The Marines sustained 23,753 total casualties, or about 33 percent of their available force. These are the true heroes. I am merely a survivor.

There have been many times I wished I could somehow erase from my mind those events I witnessed during that crucial time in history. I know you will understand this as you read on. And yet strangely now at 84 years old, I feel it is by God's grace that I am still able to recall in such detail the "Hell on

Earth" on the island of Iwo Jima February 19th, 1945, through March 26th, 1945.

So here goes – lean back in your chair and try to follow me as I write my epitaph. I am simply an ordinary person with an extraordinary story that I must tell and America must never forget!

Cpl. Marion F. Walker
Headquarters Company
2nd Battalion
28th Regiment
5th Marine Division
#906419

Frank Walker in his office at home

FORWARD

BY BECKY WHITE, CO-AUTHOR

For those of you who paid shamefully little attention in history class (like me), let me briefly recap the history and the price of World War II, as taken from bits and pieces of information I was able to garner from sources on the internet.

First, you need to remember that in WWII, the major Axis powers (or force) were Germany, Japan, and Italy. The Allied powers were those countries opposed to the Axis powers, mainly Britain, USSR, and the U.S., known as the "Big Three." Franklin Roosevelt referred to the Big Three and China as the "Four Policemen."

Here is an abbreviated synopsis of the timeline of World War II:

In 1939, Germany, led by Chancellor Adolph Hitler, invaded Poland, sparking war in Europe.

In May of 1940, Germany invaded France. In Britain, Winston Churchill became Prime Minister.

June 10th, 1940, Italy declared war on Britain and France; President Franklin Roosevelt declared that the U.S. will "extend to the opponents of force the material resources of this nation."

June 22nd, 1940, France signed an armistice with Germany. The French government maintained control of 2/5 of France, while Germany controlled the rest.

In early September of 1940, "The Blitz" began in London, involving all-out air raids by Germany.

September 16th, 1940, President Roosevelt authorized the first U.S. peacetime draft; all American males ages 21-36 were required to register.

September 27th, 1940, Japan joined the Axis power of Germany and Italy. The three nations agreed to provide military and economic assistance to one another. They are opposed by the Allies: Britain, France, the U.S.S.R., and the United States.

November 5th, 1940, Franklin D. Roosevelt won an unprecedented third term election as President of the United States.

June 22nd, 1941, Germany invaded the Soviet Union.

December 7th, 1941, Japan launched a surprise attack on Pearl Harbor, killing 2,400 people and sinking eight battleships. At the same time, Hitler issued the "Night and Fog" policy, authorizing the disappearance of "persons endangering German security."

December 8th, 1941, the U.S. declared war on Japan.

December 11th, 1941, Italy and Germany declared war on the United States.

May 12th, 1942, Hitler ordered the first mass gassing of Jews at the Auschwitz Concentration Camp in Germany.

June 4th-6th, 1942, the U.S. defeated Japanese forces in the Battle of Midway, marking the first major U.S. victory in the Pacific war.

August 7th, 1942, American troops landed on Guadalcanal, the largest of the Solomon Islands in the Pacific.

January 14th-24th, 1943, at a conference in Casablanca, Morocco, Roosevelt and Churchill agreed to prepare for the invasion of France and demand the unconditional surrender of the Axis powers.

January 31st, 1943, German forces surrendered at Stalingrad, marking the turning point of the war in Eastern Europe.

January 25th, 1944, the German commander in Poland reports that of the 2.5 million Jews originally under his jurisdiction, all but 100,000 had been killed.

June 6th, 1944, more than 150,000 Allied troops, including 13,000 U.S. paratroopers, landed in France on D-Day.

August 25th, 1944, Allies liberated Paris which had been under German control since 1940.

November 7th, 1944, Franklin D. Roosevelt is re-elected to an unprecedented fourth term as U.S. President.

December 16th, 1944, Germany launched the Battle of the Bulge in Belgium. The Allies were victorious in this battle, which ended on January 28th, 1945.

February 4th-11th, 1945, Roosevelt, Churchill and Joseph Stalin met at the Yalta conference to reapportion post-war Europe, leaving most of Eastern Europe under Soviet control.

February 19th – March 26th, 1945, in one of war's costliest offensives, the U.S. captured the island of Iwo Jima.

April 1st – June 23rd, 1945, the Battle of Okinawa.

On April 12th, 1945, President Roosevelt died, and Harry S. Truman became the 33rd President of the U.S.

April 30th, 1945, Adolph Hitler committed suicide.

May 8th, 1945, Germany surrendered unconditionally to the Allies.

August 6th, 1945, the U.S. dropped an atomic bomb on Hiroshima, Japan.

August 9th, 1945, the U.S. dropped a second atomic bomb on Nagasaki, Japan.

August 15th, 1945, Japan accepted the Allies' terms of surrender, effectively ending WWII.

So World War II began in September of 1939 when one insane leader, Adolph Hitler led Germany in an invasion of Poland, sparking war in Europe and throughout the world. World War II finally ended in August of 1945, bringing to an end six years of world-wide chaos and war, and claiming an estimated loss of between **61 and 73 MILLION lives!**

President Roosevelt died of a stroke on April 12th, 1945, undoubtedly brought on by the extreme pressure from WWII and the tough decisions he had to make.

Adolph Hitler committed suicide on April 30th, 1945. An estimated **5,830,000** Jews had been tortured and murdered at concentration camps under his leadership. Germany surrendered unconditionally to the Allies on May 8th, 1945.

Japan's Prime Minister Tojo, (nicknamed "Razor Tojo") who led his country into WWII with the surprise attack on Pearl Harbor in December of 1941, attempted suicide in September of 1945 to avoid arrest by the Occupation authorities. He was found guilty of war crimes by the Tokyo Tribunal and was hanged on December 23rd, 1948.

My hope is that as you read this book, the scenes depicted within these pages will invoke emotions that will serve as a constant reminder to you of the price that has been paid for our nation to be the awesome country that it is today. My wish is that as you see our red, white, and blue flag, known as Old Glory, majestically waving in the wind, or hear "The Star-Spangled Banner," that you will feel a renewed sense of patriotism and deep gratitude for the many blessings we have inherited. Those blessings have come with a hefty price tag to so many, and that is a fact we must never forget. May we, the citizens of the United States of America, forever remember the cost of the rich freedom we enjoy and yet be ever vigilant of those who would seek to destroy us. And may God bless America!

PREFACE

Recently, on a very cold, miserable evening in the dead of
winter in Indiana, I was spending a few moments with my
good friend and fellow veteran, Louie Hallett, and I asked
him, "Would you go through another Korean and Vietnam
war in your life?"

He looked at me and said, "In a heartbeat."

I peered back at him and asked, "Why?"

With tears streaming down the ruddy lines in his aged and
weathered face, he said, "Because I love America."

In those four words he caught the real meaning of patriotism
and why I am writing this book.

Because I love America.

CHAPTER ONE
MY BEGINNING

When I came into this world on July 9th, 1925, my little town of North Salem, Indiana, didn't order a big parade, but my mother and dad and four year old sister were just as proud. My only sibling was my sister, Ramona, who was named from the book "Ramona" about an Indian girl. Mom and Dad gave me the name of Marion Franklin, the same name as an itinerant preacher by whose demeanor they were smitten. My mother's name before marrying my dad was Grace Dexter Booker, coming from a little town in Jackson County, Indiana, called Medora. My dad was from a family named Walker who settled in North Salem in Hendricks County, Indiana. Our Walker ancestry dates back to Sir Frances Drake in age old England. My grandmother and grandfather settled in North Salem, Indiana, and that little town has become a pivotal point in my life. Back in those days, it had a population of 511, plus or minus a very few. According to the census taken in 2000, the population was 591. Apparently in the 75 years following my birth, there has been a population boom of 80 people! For me, that town has become the Alpha and Omega of my life, in that it was my beginning and will be my end. In remembering my past, I am reminded of an age-old poem:

Backward, turn backward, o time in thy flight,
Turn back a century just for tonight.
Turn back the cycles of months and years,
That all may see glimpses of joys and tears,
Of sorrows, of struggles, of pleasures and care,
Let's look friends and neighbors at what's written there.
Let's view this brave struggle, and God give us grace
To preserve and to cherish what time would efface.
Backward, turn backward, O time in thy flight,
Turn back a century just for tonight,
Their mark of events let us view with one mind,
With prejudice, envy and malice behind.
Let's glean from it lessons of friendship forsooth,
The lessons of kindness, of unselfish truth,
Let's think of ourselves in time's measureless span,
As only a part in a God-given plan.

---Grace Duckworth

The generations of today hear our stories about Americans living through the "Great Depression" during the 1930's, and seem to wonder in near disbelief how we survived those years. It seems many of our new "affluent society", who have been given everything both by government and family, can't quite understand the wealth of soul and character that is so often formed through hardships. We, who are now in our 80's, tell about taking our Saturday night baths in a large pan behind a pot-bellied stove. In hindsight, that bar of Life-buoy soap could do wonders! We describe the "outhouse" with the good ole Sears and Roebuck catalog. When we talk about our two room school (sometimes only one), they wonder where we sat the computer!! The thing this new generation does not seem to grasp is that those were in many ways the richest years of our lives, and laid a solid foundation in preparing us for the rain which was bound to come.

I grew up knowing that helping to care for the five acres that my family owned in the country out from Seymour, Indiana, was part of my responsibility. Every square foot that wasn't gardened was used to either raise hogs or chickens. These were the Depression years when we grew most of our food, and never was anything thrown away. As a young boy, I spent hours straightening crooked, rusty nails because they could be used later (and they were!)

During the springs and summers, my sister and I, along with Mom and Dad, would hoe, plant, seed and cultivate our garden until dark. In the late summer and early fall months, the four of us would work side-by-side harvesting, cleaning, and canning our produce on our old woodstove. Then about midnight we would fall into bed so my mother could go to work at the Reliance Shirt Factory in Seymour. She made 38 cents an hour. My dad, who worked as a carpenter and paper hanger, would paper an entire 15 square foot living room for $4.00. Even though people had very little money (even the bankers were broke), they could always find the $4.00 to help give their lives a glimmer of sunshine in their home. Incidentally, the charge of $4.00 back then would cost about $150 to have it done now.

I must tell you about Porky the pig. This pig deserves more than an honorable mention because of his personality.

I grew up understanding that God had made all living creatures. This particular being found himself at a great disadvantage early in life because his mother (the sow) had only so many faucets and poor Porky was left out. But he, being very clever, rolled his eyes up at my dad and said, "Mr. Walker, what can I do? Can you help me?" Of course Dad, who had a way of communicating with animals, somehow spoke in piggy language, "Yes, I'll help." That pig grew up never knowing he was a pig. In his mind, he was one of us! Porky followed us wherever we went – in the garden, on the porch, even in the kitchen, oinking up a blue streak! He received a bath every other day in a tub on the back porch and enjoyed every moment of it. My sister, Ramona, thought this was so disgusting, but we loved that guy. Dad fashioned a home for him out of an old washing machine tub. Every night Dad would go out and set this "house" on top of him. But as Porky began to grow, we would look out the kitchen window and see that house moving across the yard. Seems Porky had outgrown the door of his house. One of us would go out to rescue him and that guy pig always said "Thank you" with his oink-oinks. Can you not help but love this character? Finally, after about three years, we perhaps had overfed him and he passed away. But he would always remain in our memory.

And then there was Billy Whiskers, the goat. Probably most who are reading this have never raised a goat. If you have, you will surely agree that their minds are much like a human's, and I dare say maybe even better. They, by nature, are mischievous and always show it. Billy Whiskers was Dad's goat because Dad was the only one who could control him. Billy was strong!

Dad had built a red two-wheeled cart with a harness that Billy loved to pull behind him. Now Billy had one major flaw of character: he had a foul mouth. Where he picked up this language, we never knew; but he always used it to his advantage. His accentuated "Bleep, bleep – BLEEP, BLEEP", along with his adamant body language led us to understand his curse words, which he knew how and when to use.

When we were all going to be away, we had a metal stake driven out in a grassy area where he would stay until we got home. This one day he jumped up and ran in circles around that stake, let out a few cuss words and looked mad, then laid down on a burlap sack. After a few minutes, he performed the same scene all over. Finally we went out to see why Billy was acting so berserk. We knew the guy had no hard liquor or anything. What we discovered was a large battalion of red ants underneath that sack; and that was what was causing Billy to loose his Christianity!

Dad had built a garage and had lined the entire south exposure with Model-T Ford windshield glass from a local junk yard. The glass pieces were all of equal straight dimensions and his work bench was placed inside under the glass. Billy had the run of the five acres, and whenever he wanted to, he would climb up on the bench in the sun and go to sleep. One time Dad took a flat board and came down hard on one end of the bench. Billy jumped out and said, "Son of a bleep!" and took out every one of those eight pieces of windshield glass. After all that was happening to him, every time one of us would pick up a board, Billy would shuffle his feet and let out his familiar "Bleep, bleep" saying, "You're not going to do that to me again!"

So what ever happened to Billy Whiskers? There was a family named Hallett about a mile away who had several boys, and they were even poorer than most of us. So Dad gave Billy to that family for company. Today, all these years later, Louis Hallett and I remain good friends. He has survived the Korean and Vietnam Wars, and we see each other from time to time at Walmart in Seymour. You may wonder what happened to our beloved Billy Whiskers. These were Depression years and they butchered him for meat. Enough said!

7

In most rural communities in America, there can be found people who become very dear to your heart. This is the legacy of Mertie and Tom Covert, two tremendous individuals.

To begin with, Tom had a severely profane mouth, and when excited, he used it freely. Now Mertie, his wife, was in the Ladies Aid Society and was involved in every club and well-doing project the church had to offer. They lived about 800 yards behind the church. To Tom, that church should have been torn down and, in his words, "Maybe, just maybe, the new building could be filled up with 'good people' and not hypocrites." Then his mouth would spew out all of the usual familiar curse words and even some he had made up.

You might think that everyone would despise him, but that just wasn't the case. Everyone loved him. If anyone needed anything, Tom was there. He was a very giving person, not because he had to be, but only because he wanted to be. That was what made Tom …. Tom.

Now Mertie was another kind of individual. To be around her even just five minutes was an unforgettable experience. If you were feeling as low as a cat's belly, you would be laughing within five minutes with her. She acted as mid-wife to so many young women who found themselves "in that way." Her favorite thing was to bake bread and have Tom take it around to those she knew would need it. You could smell the wonderful aroma coming from her kitchen for a mile away.

One day Mertie decided she was going to learn to drive. Their transportation was an old Model-T Ford pickup truck.

For those of you too young to remember these classic old automobiles, you must understand that to drive a Model-T you needed to be double-jointed, know what made the thing move, and make sure you went to the bathroom before you began your journey. In other words, it was an experience!

So Mertie got in (I should say got on), and had Tom crank it up. If the thing would backfire, it would throw your shoulder out of place for a week. Ah yes, those were the days!

She pulled down on the spark lever, and of course this breathed new life into that old machine. You could almost see blue flames coming out of the rear end that would be similar to a dinosaur getting ready for a sexual encounter. This ole truck was READY! She took her foot off the brake and it shot forward! The first thing in her path was a stack of straw. She hit that pile head-on and all you could see was straw flying through the air! She emerged on the other side still hanging on and yelling, "Tom, get out of the way! Shut this darn thing off!!"

Tom was spewing chewing tobacco out of his mouth and trying to come up with another cuss word. The next thing in her path was the hen house. She hit that ole building broadside and the whole thing collapsed. She hadn't gathered the eggs yet and it became a slippery mess. Most of the eggs landed on her bosom. Chickens were flying through the air and lost their feathers en route. She made a big circle around the house with poor Tom behind trying to catch up. He never made it and Mertie was aimed at a big pile of watermelons in the front yard that were for sale. This old Ford just kept gaining new life because she had the spark lever all the way down. She hit those watermelons square on! You can imagine how she looked covered with broken eggs and watermelons. By this time, Mertie had lost her Christianity and she picked up some of Tom's profanity. Poor guy, he could not catch her.

She found herself aimed at the dilapidated fence where they kept the hogs. She ripped a hole in it (which was easy to do) and the next thing in her path was a lean-to used as a hog house. The hogs, who were busy eating, saw her coming and began to scatter. Even those pigs had developed Tom's cuss words. She missed them all, but their house was on the ground, demolished! The noise and racket was unbelievable! By this time, she had lost the fenders and the rotten bed on the truck which by now looked like a skeleton. She had hit one of their geese and completely de-feathered it!

Next stop… the old barn which housed a mule that had seen its better day. Mertie hit that barn and one side of it fell down. That old mule took off – he hadn't traveled that fast for years! We located him in the cemetery ¼ mile away. He probably thought, "If I'm going to die, it might as well be in a cemetery!" And from that point on, he would pin his ears back and glare at Mertie every time he saw her!

Well, there was only one building left and that was Tom and Mertie's house! They had a cistern in the backyard from which they pulled water for their livestock. The poor old truck hit the cistern at a glance, fell in, and one wheel broke off. The ordeal was finally over and Mertie climbed out of her seat and declared, "I believe we need a new truck!" Tom was sick from swallowing his "chew"

Mertie came over to the restaurant and told the folks there of her adventure. Within hours, their place was a beehive of activity with men from the pumping station and neighbors to rebuild what had been ripped asunder in a matter of a few minutes.

Tom wound up getting a Model-A Ford and Mertie, with help, learned to drive. For those of us who were connected to them, even after many years, it was so good to talk about that unforgettable incident.

Is it any wonder that Mertie and Tom Covert were very special to the people who knew them?

Bill Richmond, the local preacher, declared the next Sunday that if Tom and Mertie had been Christians, this incident would never have happened to them. Bill had implored Tom to come to church, but made it clear that before he did he needed to straighten up his mouth. Tom thought that over and told him (in his usual colorful language), "I wouldn't be caught dead with you there!" It so happened that Pastor Richmond did not last long after that. Wonder why?

Life was so good and so simple as I was growing up. Throughout my adult life I have often looked back with amazement at the ability of my mother and dad as they went through life, and in most cases, they went through life with ease. Why? They learned early in their life that you make the tomorrow – today. They had learned you never wait until the next day when a calamity might happen. They were always prepared for the next day before it happened. And this ability to cope has certainly followed me as I have gone through life.

My father never went beyond the eighth grade in school. This was not uncommon for boys growing up in that generation. So he didn't possess any great degree of "book learning." But somehow he could take an ordinary carpenter's square and tell you within one minute how long the rafters would have to be (in building a house), what the angle would be as two rafters met each other, what the angle would be as that rafter formed the correct fit onto the plate of the house, and how many inches the roof would be from the "comb" of the roof, down to and including the eave extension. All of this information was coming from that carpenter's square. This information didn't show on that square, it only had inches indented into it. Now how he did it, I do not know. He had explained it many times to me, but I was unable to pick it up, even though math was my better course in high school. The amazing thing about this is that he never missed. He was always correct.

Consider this ability with the carpenters of today. Their rafters are pre-cut, assembled at a factory, and shipped in by truck. In Dad's day, the studding and rafters were made of hard oak, cut only with a hand saw. Now an electric cutoff saw is the norm. They were 2 x 4's, and not a cut down version of the same. Is it any wonder that my dad stood a mile high in my estimation of him? His intelligence and ability came from experience and not off the internet or a calculator which do the thinking for you. Dad's entire life was an example of using the intelligence that God had given him. And because of this, I grew up with nothing but the greatest respect for him and Mom. They were the example, and my sister and I learned from them every day.

My mother exhibited this ability in yet another way. If a pair of socks had a hole in them, she would darn them by hand and extend the life of them by six months. Unlike today, she didn't get in the car and drive to Walmart, paying $4.00 for a gallon of gasoline to buy a $2.00 pair of socks.

Even though my mother had a few cookbooks, she never used them. Neither do I, and I have been cooking for 70 years. She would throw in a little of this and a little of that. It was always the "that" which became the surprise of the day – <u>always</u> an enjoyable surprise. Why follow a cookbook when you know as much as the person who wrote it? This was her philosophy. Of course that idea might have been in contradiction to her former few years, when she had been a school teacher and taught out of a book. Oh well!

In the spring, summer, and fall, our kitchen resembled a canning factory of today. All of this took place either on weekends or at night because she worked at a shirt factory in Seymour for several years making $.38 an hour. Everything in that kitchen operated like a machine, and when the labor was done, she would stand back and say, "Look at those beautiful peaches!" (or whatever we were canning) There was never a can of vegetables that were canned in Mexico or China!! We grew and canned our own veggies and fruit. Therein lies the difference of yesterday and today.

It is no wonder we have become a "gimme" society. The younger generations of today are missing so much in having everything given to them. A can of homegrown peaches is so much better than those found in our modern day grocery departments. Backward, turn backwards, oh time in thy flight! We of today are missing so much by not returning to the family values that meant so much in those years. We are so engrossed in those things which we think will make us happy, if only for a fleeting moment. But it is that "fleeting moment" mentality that has made us pure lazy and our lives without value. No wonder my generation recalls so many of their family values that have meant so much to them. Everyone I talk to of that generation have such good memories of those years interspersed with some hard times. And yes, those hard times are important in our lives, too.

These are just a few memorable stories that reverberate in my memory of childhood in the small town where I grew up. Along with those memories is a section of my life that was centered on a place called Pauley's Camp which was located on the White River, about ½ mile from home. How I loved that place and because of it, I want to spend some time there with you.

Chapter Two
Pauley's Camp
and the Indian Mound

The Indian Mound as it stands today. Frank and his father helped with the construction of the monument commemorating the battle between the native Americans and General John Tipton

It would be nice if every child in America could grow up in a place like Pauley's Camp. Such was my privilege. Unlike today, it was not a time when you had to be afraid for your very being. Located on the White River, it was about ten mostly wooded acres that could have been called the most beautiful spot in southern Indiana. My dad and I were privileged to help in making it so.

The property belonged to Charley and Laura Pauley who had a vision of what the property could become. Because my dad was self-employed and lived nearby, he was a natural for the work at Pauley's Camp. So with the Pauleys' vision and financial means, and my dad's expertise and ingenuity to make it happen, their dream became a reality.

There was a bit of history connected to the property called The Indian Mound.

Way back before Indiana became a state, the whole area belonged to the Indians. But lo and behold, we (the government), being expansionists had to kill off the Indians and usurp the territory. Oh yes, have we always been angels? I think not.

There is a tiny island about 500 yards up White River where the river separates, forming an island in the middle. General John Tipton, whose father had been killed by a Native American, chased the Indians off this land, got them cornered on the tiny island and massacred most of them. This story is in all the Indiana history books.

The Indian custom was to bury their dead on top of the ground, so when the attack was over, the few surviving Indians carried dirt in to cover their loved ones, and to this day that pile of dirt is called the Indian Mound. This battle took place very near the acres that we owned at one time. After a century and a-half, we were still picking up arrow flints. Steve Gill from Seymour owns property behind the Mound and found a tomahawk just recently.

Charley Pauley, having a soft heart and interest in history, wanted to build a monument on top. My dad poured the cement and I did what I could as a kid to help construct the monument which became the focal point of Pauley's Camp.

All through the 1930's, the camp grew in notoriety as a weekend retreat for those from Indianapolis, Chicago, and all around who wanted to "get away from it all." Through those years, Dad had built a total of 16 rustic cabins and the dance pavilion, and still found time to construct a new house for our family.

The cabins were all made of native rough-sawed lumber with a kitchen area and a loft in the upper level. Most had running water in the kitchen sink, but everyone used communal outhouses. Throughout the woods were scattered walking trails and roasting pits for hot dogs. It was a Mecca for squirrels, and woe to the man who came into the woods with a shotgun. As a result, most of the chipmunks and squirrels became pets and the public loved every moment of it.

Dad had built a huge pavilion where dances with top bands were held every Friday and Saturday night. The building had very few windows. Instead, the sides of the buildings had hinges which were raised up to make it an open-air pavilion. There was no air conditioning back in the 1930's!

The nights when our family would choose not to go over, we would sit on our front porch and listen to the sweetest music this side of Heaven!

Even though Charley Pauley himself would occasionally imbibe, I would often see him sitting at the gate to all of this Mecca and promise to shoot anyone who attempted to bring a bottle onto his premises. As a result, the camp became known far and wide as a perfect retreat. My dad had such a great part in it and I learned so many lessons from the whole experience that it's no wonder that Pauley's Camp still, to this day, carries such memories for me.

I am so appreciative of those hours I spent fishing with a string dangling from a willow pole, or just watching the water flow south on White River while observing nature at its best, being influenced by Charley and Laura Pauley, meeting people who were the "salt of the earth". What a solid foundation was laid for my life!

As I reflect back on my life and contemplate those years rich with memories, it is certainly true that those years of living through the Great Depression, the Pauley's Camp years, the years spent with Mom and Dad on our five acres with garden and livestock, the love and the respect that we had for each other, was preparing me for the rain which was bound to come on Iwo Jima.

Although my sister Ramona was the recipient of the family love that existed, she perhaps did not respond the way I did. This is not to take anything from Ramona, she was just a different personality. She was an A+ student and an accomplished musician (clarinet). She had her own group of friends in town and they might have been her driving force. She had a burning desire to "give back" through nursing. This was the force that drove her.

Mom and Dad took out a heavy mortgage on our five acres to send her to the Bethesda Hospital School of Nursing in Cincinnati, Ohio, a career she followed her entire life. Later in her life, she served as a County Health Nurse for many years.

During those years, I would try to make it home from Florida or California on Thanksgiving or Christmas. Many times she would spend two days before these holidays cooking and baking. The day before the holiday, I would go with her throughout the county delivering her pre-cooked meals to those in dire need. Because she was the Health Nurse, she was aware of who was in need and where they lived. This was my sister, Ramona. She didn't have to do that, it certainly was not connected to her job whatsoever, but it was just her way to "give back." The values our mom and dad had projected during our formative years certainly reflected in her life.

Sadly, later in her life, she became dependent on medical drugs and her entire personality changed. Is it any wonder that I am totally against pharmaceuticals?

Ramona was extremely proud of me, her younger and only brother, as I joined the U.S. Marine Corps. She loved America and to her, having a brother in the U.S. Marines was her joy. She could quote every Walker name that was in combat for our country since Sir Francis Drake and the Revolutionary War – and there were many!

Frank with his father who was wearing his 1918 uniform

CHAPTER THREE
AMERICA'S WAKE-UP CALL
DECEMBER 7TH, 1941

On December 7th, 1941, the attack on Pearl Harbor by Japan took place. Suddenly the whole world changed. Our peaceful lives became topsy-turvy, and it all happened so fast! Planes from Japanese aircraft carriers bombed and torpedoed the U.S. naval fleet stationed in Hawaii and attacked airfields on the island. The next day the United States declared war on Japan, entering World War II.

How could we as a nation describe our emotions? This was America being attacked from without. Whether you were a Democrat or Republican, it made no difference. On December 8th, when President Roosevelt had a chance to talk to us as a nation via radio, we all wondered, "What does all of this mean?"

To begin with, most of the country (including myself still in high school) did not even know where Pearl Harbor was. Naturally, there were no televisions, since TV's didn't hit the market until 1958. For those of us living in rural areas, even newspapers were scarce. Telephones were practically useless because throughout rural America, telephones operated via party lines. We would crank up four short rings to reach Violet at the Office Central in Reddington. After four rings, you would have to wait and wait for her to pick up because she might be in the outside privy or washing her unmentionables. This was rural America, circa 1941 and 1942.

At this time, most families in America were recuperating from the horrible Depression and most of us felt that if we were able to open our eyes early in the morning, it must be a good day. The truth is that we as a nation were not ready for this. Some of the young men had enlisted in the Army because Hitler was on the rampage. But the full impact of war did not hit home for several days. We did not understand the Japanese and their expansion plans in the Pacific.

Back in those years, just prior to December 7th, we in the country would sell scrap metal to a "junk man" coming through town. He would pay us three cents per pound for any metal we had. For us growing up, this was a tidy sum since it didn't take much junk to make ten pounds. It never dawned on us that that same metal was being thrown back at us from Japan who we considered to be a friend. Boy, were we mistaken! Japan was shooting at us with the same metal we had sold them just a few months before.

Franklin D. Roosevelt's words rang true… "This day will long live in infamy!" In less than two hours, the Japanese military had all but wiped out our entire Navy. The United States Air Corps was in its infancy, but was blown clear off the map at Pearl Harbor and Henderson Field, in the Hawaiian Islands.

At the same time, German submarines were coming right into New York Harbor, Boston Harbor, and Charleston Harbor. In other words, we as a nation were caught off guard. While our generals and admirals were arguing what to do, President Roosevelt, being the leader that he was, said, "Don't tell me we can't win this thing! We are going to do it. Not later, but NOW!" And overnight the country began to change. Political parties sat aside their differences and pulled together for the benefit of the country. It was America, now and forever. We discovered for our own survival, that we were fighting two wars at the same time – one in the Atlantic and one in the Pacific. Roosevelt tried his best to stay out of Europe, but discovered that we had to become embroiled in the Hitler takeover.

The two countries, Japan and Germany, were feeding off each other. It had to be a two-front war. Was America prepared? No, we were not; but thanks to a powerful president, our image of ourselves changed at once.

The change was even taking place in our schools. In most of the classrooms in high school, before we would hit the books, we, along with the teacher, would spend a few minutes on current events. And in Social Studies, we were given extra credit for bringing in as many newspaper clippings as we could find to discuss in the class. Much of our news would come from the beginning of the movies we were about to see at the Vondee or Majestic theater in Seymour. Those were the days of some top reporters like Edward R. Murrow and K. V. Kaltenborn who reported the news as it happened, not what they thought would make a good story. And then, of course, a little later came Walter Winchell and many others. It was upon this setting that students of all ages in school became aware of the events happening around them, in their families, and all over the world.

This was such a turning point in history, not only for America, but for the whole world. It disturbs me that in many of today's high school history books only four pages are devoted to World War II, and the Pacific Theater of the war is scarcely mentioned at all!

George Santayna has said, "Those who cannot learn from history are doomed to repeat it." And so for those who have not learned, I am sharing my story which the current history books have for some reason omitted, so that hopefully the horrors of WWII will not be repeated!

John F. Kennedy is quoted as saying in his Inaugural Address in 1961:

"...Let the word go forth, that the torch has been passed to a new generation of Americans.

"Let every nation know that we shall pay any price, bear any burden, meet any hardship, support any friend, oppose any foe, in order to assure the survival and the success of liberty."

And this unforgettable quote from that same speech:

"And so my fellow Americans, ask not what your country can do for you, ask what you can do for your country."

But here we are in the year 2009/2010, and the younger generation seemingly knows nothing about those years. And many, by their own admission, couldn't care less. As a member of the older generation, it makes me cringe and cry out that we have raised a self-serving and indulgent generation. Some belong to religious creeds who spend their time discussing what color underwear John the Baptist wore! And if they are on drugs, and so many are, they are wondering how to get another "hit." This behavior grieves me greatly, and I wonder and worry about the future of America.

The war effort began hitting home as men and women started working at Allison's in Indianapolis making aircraft engines. The people in Anderson, Muncie, and Kokomo areas were laboring day and night producing tanks. Folks from Jeffersonville and New Albany areas were making Higgins boats, which were landing crafts that could ferry as many as 36 soldiers to shore.

Suddenly the items that we all thought essential, such as tires, gasoline, cans, sugar, etc., became non-existent. Our world changed so fast!

Within three months after that historical day, a corporation from Texas named Texas Eastern was building a pipeline from

Texas to the east coast of America, which was to be thousands of miles long. This pipeline was being built to carry oil and gas across the nation, which was crucial to the war effort. One of their pumping stations was located just one mile from Reddington, my home territory. My family had opened a restaurant and gas station on U.S. Highway 31. The workers who were building the pumping station would eat two meals a day there with Mom cooking and Dad and I waiting tables. There were three shifts of workers from the pumping station, so we had to hire help. Remember Mertie Covert, the lady who wreaked havoc trying to drive the Model- T pickup truck? She made all of our homemade pies at the restaurant. The Texas Eastern men were wild about them! The price for a big piece of pie with a cup of coffee: 25¢!

During this time I learned how to cook for a large number of people, a skill that would serve me well in time to come. The pipeline workers were a terrific crew and they appreciated us being open for them. The whole episode shows how fast America became mobilized, really just overnight.

December 7, 1941, so unbelievable, but it happened, and President Roosevelt proclaimed in one of his fireside chats to the nation: "This day will long live in infamy!"

Japanese Imperial Admiral Yamamoto, who conceived, designed and promoted the Pearl Harbor attack, cautioned against a war with the United States. Having twice held naval positions within the Japanese embassy in the U.S. Capitol, he knew well the industrial strength, material wealth and temperament of the U.S. Overruled by his superiors, he dedicated his efforts as Commander in Chief of the Japanese Fleets to a successful attack. Upon completion of the attack, he is quoted as saying, "We have awakened a sleeping giant and have instilled in him a terrible resolve."

How true his words were. And this day set my life on a new course, namely my life leading to the U.S. Marine Corps and the Battle of Iwo Jima, the place so appropriately named "Hell on Earth."

CHAPTER FOUR
MY ENLISTMENT

Frank with his proud mother and father

Seymour, Indiana, was a quaint town of maybe six to seven thousand people in December of 1941. However, within weeks of the bombing at Pearl Harbor, our government had bought up or leased hundreds of acres just south of Seymour. Much of it was owned by the Schneck family who had become quite wealthy by raising horseradish, of all things. Hence the name of our current hospital, the Schneck Memorial Hospital, came into being.

So, after the government took over this land, runways suddenly appeared where cornfields used to be, and buildings went up as thousands of young men came into town to become a part of the country's new Air Force. This was the beginning of Freeman Air Field which still exists today, but is no longer a military operation.

Platter's Photography became more than just a place to buy film. It was now a place for the young airmen to sit for a picture to be sent home. Gas stations went up – Shell, Sinclair, Texaco, Gulf – instead of just Hoosier Pete's gas, which was eight gallons for $1.00.

The G. C. Murphy Dime Store grew to where they took over two adjoining rooms. Yes, Seymour and all of America was on the move! It was this kind of dynamics in our hometown Seymour that caused so many 17 year olds to want to hurry up time so they could be 18 years old and be part of America at war.

And so, enter Frank Walker. All through high school I was on the academic courses for my studies, which included two years of Latin, all of the mathematics I could get (including trigonometry and a bit of calculus), history, social studies, etc. I trudged through most of 1942 fully expecting and wanting to enter Rose Polytechnic Institute in Terre Haute, Indiana, for an engineering degree and would come out a 2nd Lieutenant. I even enrolled, but backed out during the last week. I just knew I had to be a U. S. Marine. Dad understood, but I doubt that Mom did.

Enlisting with the Marines was just not as exciting as enrolling at a University, and Mom knew, as did I, there was grave danger ahead in the military. My desire to enlist was certainly not because of the uniform, even though the girls would go crazy over that. It was, and still is, a deep abiding love for America, and the ideology that came from my dad. I knew what caused Dad in those early years to stand and salute our flag as it went by. As a young boy, I had watched and understood as his lower lip quivered and tears rolled down his cheeks at the sight of "Old Glory." I perceived that he knew what had made America so great. And I also knew his deep

31

belief in our country brought him home from the World War I battles at Chateau-Thierry and Belleau Wood, having suffered 17 different wounds. His dedication helped guide me in the direction I chose.

Because of my mother, I was able to obtain my necessary 32 credits by mid-term 1942, and graduated with three others: Bill Schulte and Don and John Maguire. With permission granted by my high-school principal, I was able to start the process of becoming a U. S. Marine at age 17.

On January 3rd, 1943, I met up with Bill Schulte, and the two of us rode the Greyhound bus into Louisville, Kentucky, where we were going to enlist in the U.S. Marine Corps. At that time the Greyhound bus would stop at every crossing, town, and city. How times have changed! As we drew closer to Louisville, the bus picked up a few boys which today would be called "men of color". I was appalled when I heard the driver of the bus say, "There's room for you darkies in the rear of the bus." To me, this was abhorrent! To me there was no difference between them and us. We were all God's children. I had not been raised to tell a difference – because there was none!

When we arrived at the bus station, the first order of business was to go to the bathroom. Immediately I saw signs which read, "Whites Only – No Blacks." My first reaction was, "Do they think the blacks have a different kind of urine and it's contaminated?" I probably shook with disbelief. Back in Seymour, this division did not exist. I began to wonder what kind of church, if any, did those people come from?

And then, while trying to recuperate from this societal shock, it was time to find something to eat. We found a small café with a lunch counter and table and chairs. Taking a seat I noticed a huge sign on the wall which read, "Whites only. All others eat outside." I guess I was beginning to wonder, "Is this America?" We were only 60 miles from home, and yet it seemed like a whole different world. My buddy, Bill, had been raised by his mother in the same type of home as I. In fact, his mother and mine worked side by side at the shirt factory in Seymour. This kind of treatment was not in our reasoning. These boys and men were there to enlist and serve America. What kind of hypocrisy was this coming out of our schools and churches? These were my thoughts and it still makes me shake with revulsion. I did not know it then, but these same men would be dying on the beach of Iwo Jima and throughout Europe unloading supplies for our troops, giving their lives for a country that treated them like I had witnessed. I began to wonder if we were trying to fight the Civil War all over. My answer to myself was and still is yes, we are, even in the year of 2010. When will it end? I believe the churches and schools have a responsibility in changing these attitudes. We can no longer wish to be "politically correct" and say nothing. It is time to end the Civil War once and for all and unite to be "All for America!" We are a nation of many colors and cultures, but we must be a <u>United</u> States of America!!

So after at least partially recuperating from this cultural shock, it was time to find the Marine Corps Enlistment Center. It was just around the corner.

We walked in and I was dumbfounded by the men in "dress blues." Oh, they showed such a display of professionalism and I knew instantly this was what I wanted. I'm sure the staff sergeant who interviewed me knew that I was only 17 years old, but could see I wanted in the Corps so badly that he passed me as 18. I was pleased that I had managed to persuade someone and he then showed me to another Marine. I thought, "Hey you guys need me – there is a war on!" I soon discovered that the Marine Corps would not enlist just anyone. If that were the case, it would not be the Marine Corps. And after all, didn't I want in because of that very reason?

After going through so many tests, I was getting tired. It started out with the chancre mechanic (Navy Corpsman slang) who checked for sexually transmitted disease. He ascertained that I was clear. (I could have told him that in the beginning!) Next was an IQ test which went like a breeze. He could not believe that I had graduated in three and a-half years from high school. He tried to tell me there was a law that mandated four years in high school. It's amazing how some with a low rank can be so stubborn.

Next came the thorough physical by a Navy doctor. He said I was in perfect health, like that was a surprise to him. Next came the psychiatrist who wanted to know why a young man such as myself wanted a military career. So, I, being grateful that I had gotten this far, decided to give him the full treatment and he was impressed (apparently).

Next came a Dress Blue Marine, which made me happy since I was getting tired of Navy. He had enough ribbons on his chest to weigh him down. I knew instantly that he was from the old school (pre-war) and I could relate to him. Of course he inquired about my experience even though I was just out of high school. I related to him how I had cooked for the pipeline workers. When he heard this, he said, "Wonderful! You are now a cook in the U.S. Marine Corps!" And I've been cooking ever since!

Finally, after an exhaustive full day, I was sworn into the Marine Corps, and I'll never forget it. During all of this process, Bill Schulte and I became separated and I never saw him again. I have heard he is living in Virginia. I'm sure that he, too, has his own story.

The enlistment read "For four years or the duration." I got my first discharge in just under four years. Then I enlisted again, which is another story.

Waiting for the next several weeks to receive my orders from the Marine Corps seemed like a lifetime. I thought, "Hey, there is a war going on! Why are you so slow?!" But the wheels of progress sometimes move slowly and my mother would say, "Have patience!" But mine was wearing thin. So finally the communication came along with travel money and the entire procedure to get to San Diego, California. "I'm now a Marine!" I declared with pride. I was wrong about that, but I didn't know it then.

So here I was, 17 years old: Marion F. Walker, United States Marine Corps, #906419, and proud of it!

The trip from Seymour, Indiana to San Diego, California by a country boy still wet behind the ears was a culture shock to say the least! There just aren't words to describe it!

Oh how I wish I had kept a diary. But I didn't, and even though the trip from Chicago to Los Angeles is fairly clear in my mind after all these many years, I'm sure there are scenes and emotions that have escaped me.

It must be remembered that so many of us "kids" were from the farm country of Indiana, Illinois, Ohio, Missouri, etc. We were not familiar with the big city of Chicago, the plains of the Midwest, or any of the western states. So the LaSalle Street Station and the hustle-bustle of the great Chicago were astounding to us. Through all of this, I did manage to get on the right train, the Santa Fe.

The troop car that was designated for me had probably been a cattle car that had been rushed to be used as a troop train. The seats were old, worn and ripped, and even some benches had been added. No carpet existed, and the filthy floors hadn't been swept for weeks. There was no heat other than a tube that blew air from Lord knows where. Remember this was still winter – cold, snowy, and freezing rain. Our engine was coal-fed, not the diesel or electric which would come about later. So every so often we would have to stop to take on water for its boiler and coal.

Pulling out of the LaSalle Street Station on the outskirts of Chicago, the war effort was very much in evidence. Factories were everywhere and you could see America on the move. Crossing the Mississippi River at St. Louis was quite an experience for me. After all, the only body of water I was familiar with was the White River in southern Indiana.

As we trudged forward, we would pick up more men (boys, really) and a new supply of outdated peanut butter and/or bologna sandwiches. Occasionally, in passing through the larger cities, volunteers of the U.S.O. or Salvation Army would run out with doughnuts or other goodies. As you can imagine, these were always appreciated by us young and hungry enlistees.

In passing through Kansas and Oklahoma, I saw thousands of acres that had been stripped of fencing and vegetation. Poor agricultural practices and years of drought in this area is what started the Dust Bowl in the 1930's, not too many years before. For eight years winds had blown across these fields causing constant billowing clouds of yellowish-brown dust to blow on these southern plains, forcing the residents to wear dust masks, and farmers to watch helplessly as their crops blew away – another remarkably distressing time in American history.

The rugged beauty of Arizona still remains in my memory and finally the state of California came into sight. While passing through California, the Santa Fe tracks led us right through an orange grove where we could (and did) reach out and pull fresh, ripe oranges right off the trees. Finally we journeyed through California's rich valleys, which had been appropriately dubbed as our country's "Salad Bowl."

Yes, even then I appreciated every mile that we covered. And because of all the geography I had seen and history I had recalled as we traveled from the heartland of Indiana to the lush valleys of California, it was then and is now so easy for me to once again proclaim, "America, I love you!"

And finally, after almost six days and nights onboard that train, the great city of Los Angeles loomed in front of us, and we were about to take our next step into the great unknown.

CHAPTER FIVE
BOOT CAMP, SAN DIEGO STYLE

All of us, as we progress through life, seem to have much better hindsight than foresight, myself included. As I am writing this, I wish I had kept a simple diary of what was happening to us in war. Back then, for whatever reason, I did not do this. Of course, the reverse of this idea would be: how are you going to write a diary with the enemy shooting, bent on the idea of killing you?! So, my recollections of those eight weeks at San Diego Marine Boot Camp are a bit sketchy and may not be in the exact order as they happened.

My whole previous life, up to this point had been built around wholesome discipline with a purpose. I went into the Marine Corps understanding they knew more than I did. This precept of life had served me well before and I knew it would continue to do so for the next four years. This is not to say that I was a "yes-man." I was not and will never be. I have always taken the First Amendment, Freedom of Speech, quite seriously.

As I stepped out of that bus onto the grounds of the Recruit Depot, I knew that a complete new life was ahead for me. After all, hadn't I enlisted because I admired the Marine Corps? So, I was ready, but very surprised. Most of us in that platoon of kids were from the heartland of America and had our heads squarely on our shoulders. We were pretty much alike. We were, however, different from those who came from the Parris Island, SC, Recruit Depot, which must have been a bit rougher.

I will highlight just a few of the events in those first hours and days of leaving civilian status to becoming a Marine. The day-to-day routine happenings I will leave for someone else to share.

First there were haircuts. I believe I was lucky, because the barber (if you can call him that) left a little more on my head than most. He might have been expecting a bribe, but he didn't get one.

Then there was the clothing which was one size – too large. We were given a scrub brush, GI soap, and a bucket to do our own laundry, and woe to the recruit that left a brown spot on the inside of the skivvies (shorts)!

We received many, many hours of orientation, which included a history of the Marine Corps dating back to its beginning, November 10, 1775.

Our new home turned out to be in tents. Sorry, no hallway with beautiful pictures on the walls. This was war and we knew it. The tents all had wooden floors and with luck, eight young Marines could be and were billeted in each unit. In every group, there is always one screw-up. So it was in our case.

I don't remember who he was or what he did, but he received a severe reprimand. Because of what he had done, the whole platoon had to suffer the consequences. We spent the entire night scrubbing each wooden floor with soap, water, and a toothbrush. Then we spent the whole next day learning how to march in unison. After that, if at any time we had a fellow Marine screw up, we came down hard on him. This idea was to serve us well at Camp Pendleton, Camp Tarawa, and later on at Iwo Jima where our very lives might depend on the Marine by our side. There was no room for screw-ups, and from that point on we had to live and work and train as one unit.

This was the very first lesson that came from those overworked Drill Instructors. Contrary to some of the movies you may have seen, these Drill Instructors were all fair. I saw in one of those Hollywood movies where the Drill Instructor was hitting and slapping the recruit. **Balderdash!** If one tried it, he would still be serving time at Alcatraz. The Marine Corps of today and all through our history is built on integrity, fairness, loyalty, commitment and character.

Concerning food, most of the platoon had been on a diet of beans and cornbread, which was so good. Of course, there is always a twit who will gripe and say, "My mother didn't cook this way." He would quickly learn to never say that in the presence of a cook. Those cooks, which I was soon to join, would come down hard on that poor recruit. It became clear that a cook considered his galley to be his territory and no one, but no one, had better insult his position, regardless of rank.

Maybe that is why these 65+ years later when I am cooking a holiday meal for our family, I want everyone out of my kitchen while I'm working! Is that the Marine Corps coming out of me after all these years? Maybe so.

As I have said previously, I will leave the day-to-day experiences to someone else. Those experiences could take up an entire book, and that is not my purpose. But it must be remembered that the Drill Instructors were given just eight weeks to transform a civilian kid into the beginning of a Marine that would be capable of killing in battle. His entire personality must be changed in that time. Some resisted it. I did not. After all, did I not give up a life of ease in college for this?

I will touch upon a few of the transformations in my life as I started boot camp.

For most of us, including myself, we had never fired a gun heavier than a .22 caliber rifle. Some may have used a 12-gauge shotgun. To become fully acclimated to our new M1 Garand .30 caliber rifle was an experience. That piece weighs close to 9 ½ pounds, and with a bayonet attached would be closer to 12 pounds. Holding that semi-automatic shoulder weapon steady at your target requires some serious practice. We soon learned it had a maximum range of 3500 yards and contained a clip holding 8 rounds. In qualifying for target, my trouble was always not taking a deep breath and exhaling. When I started, my best score was marksman, but I gradually attained the mark of sharpshooter. Expert, of course, was the best. This training was at Camp Mathews, not far from San Diego, and was a welcome week away from our usual rugged training where calisthenics with all the obstacle courses was a daily routine.

The outstanding part of the Marine Corps Boot Camp is the ability of the "boot" platoon to march in unison on the parade ground and go through all of the marching orders given by the Drill Instructor. To be a part of that platoon marching in perfect unison with the American flag in front on the parade grounds made us especially proud. To take 60+ green home kids off the streets and transform them into this was and is amazing.

Finally graduation day came. We joined other platoons on the huge parade ground and I'm sure we were a sight to behold. Whether you talked about patriotism or not, you had to feel proud to be an American. Most of us had gained 10 pounds in weight, all muscle, and we felt tremendous. After receiving a pep-talk, we were given orders as to where we were headed next. Most of us were to be sent to Camp Pendleton, up the coast at Oceanside, California, but not in all cases. We were immediately split up and boarded 6 x 6 trucks, none of us knowing where we were going. If we had started friendships with anyone in those eight weeks, it was short-lived. However, once in awhile we would run into someone we knew from boot camp.

While passing through San Diego, close to the waterfront, there was a scene that I will never forget because it depicted what America is and can be under stress. It seemed for miles there were huge factories that covered every square foot of space. Over all of these buildings were camouflage nets, so that from the air the enemy would never guess this was the largest production of aircraft in the entire world. The factories were all there – Boeing, Northrop, Piper, and Consolidated - and were producing aircraft by the thousands. How our country was able to become mobilized so fast is unbelievable. President Franklin D. Roosevelt offered the leadership to make it happen. I believe that still today the American spirit is so strong by so many that we, in a time of need, would say, "What can I do for my country, America, the country I love?" And maybe the strong would pull the weak along until we became united again!

And so, as I was passing through the beautiful city of San Diego, I knew that one chapter of my young life had ended and I was about to start a new one. As we made our journey, I gazed at countryside scenery that was entirely different from Jackson County, Indiana. I viewed orange groves as far as the eye could see. I saw farm ground consisting of thousands of acres pass before me. I observed military bases that had sprung up overnight, and beheld the Marine Corps, Navy, Coast Guard, Army, Air Corps and everything in between. I had witnessed America on the move.

Yes, I had lived through boot camp, which was notoriously horrible. I had grown from a kid in high school to the beginning of a man. These were thoughts that I had as we were bouncing over Highway 101 up the coast to Oceanside. I had lived up to my dream of becoming a U.S. Marine, even though I had miles to go.

CHAPTER SIX
CAMP PENDLETON

The entrance gate to Camp Pendleton in Oceanside, California

Camp Pendleton is one of only two main training camps for Marines in this country. The other is Camp Lejeune in North Carolina. Each base has many satellite operations which provide more specialized training scattered throughout the country, most of which are located in California and Virginia.

Camp Pendleton has a unique part in the history of our country, especially California. It was originally purchased in 1942, containing 125,000 acres which was only the southern half of a huge ranch, the second largest in the world. The largest was the King Ranch in Hawaii. The price? $4.25 million ($34.00 per acre). Located between San Diego and Orange County, it included 17 miles of undeveloped beachfront property, valuable ranch land, and scenic landscape. As you can imagine, today's real estate developers would die for this property. It has passed through several owners over the many years, but became known as the Santa Margarita Rancho. Other names over the many years (since 1769) were landmarks known as Rattlesnake Canyon, Harno Canyon and Las Pulgas Canyon, so named for the fleas that infested the area. These fleas are still there today and are so big they wear Marine Corps uniforms!! The part of the ranch that belongs to the U.S. Marines stretches from the San Luis Valley, which touches the outskirts of Oceanside, all the way up the coast to El Toro, or about 35 miles. At its widest point, it is about 15 miles, which is right up against the cities of Vista and Escondido. Most of the old ranch buildings are still standing and are part of the California historical sites. They are all built in the old Spanish Hacienda style which adds to the flavor of this tremendous acreage.

About eight miles from the old original Ranch House is the Los Flores Adobe built in 1865 by one of the owners. The Adobe has its own romantic history. If you will remember, I told of my sister Ramona being named after an Indian girl mentioned in a book by the author Helen Hunt Jackson. Helen had lived at Los Flores for a time and had based her novel upon the people she met and the places at the ranch. All of this would lead you to believe the book was not fictional, but reality. The buildings, history, and legacy are being preserved by the Marine Corps and many other interested parties.

It has been 66 years since I was there, and I feel privileged to have been a part of the history of Camp Pendleton where more than 50,000 Marines and civilians are stationed today. It has become a national and state treasure. That base was my home for so long. We even managed to co-exist with the rattlesnakes in the hills.

But to understand Camp Pendleton, you must come with me as I recall my life at the camp. The existence of part of its acreage has over the years become the object of many who would tear it apart, but the Marines have come up fighting every time. Yes, we did lose a couple miles of coastline to the do-gooders in politics; but in the whole, Camp Pendleton is still intact. Just to give you a little history, the politicians in Oceanside were refusing to educate the Marines' children, so what did General Erskine do? He built our own schoolhouse which is still operating today. The irony of the many battles was that the very Marines who had enlisted to protect the populace were being shoved aside by these same people. Sometimes we have to wonder what is going on in the America we love. I'm sure I'll touch upon this as I continue to write.

Coming to the gate which reads, "Camp Pendleton, Home of the U. S. Marines – West Coast," we were motioned through by the guard. At this point, we in the 6 x 6 truck had no idea of what was in store for us. It turned out to be the crucible of our lives until we hit the island of Iwo Jima. It was here that the separation of the boys from the men began at a fast pace. We soon learned there was no place in the Marine Corps for those who were not up to the challenge; in fact, we didn't even have the chance to say goodbye to those unfortunates.

After bouncing around in the back of that 6 x 6 truck, over nothing but a trail for a road, down a gulley, up a cliff, seeing jack rabbits scurrying away, we arrived at a flat area that had been scraped out of this no-man's land. Remember, Camp Pendleton was just over one year old at this time, and the

Japanese were trying to kill us at Guadalcanal, Bougainville, and the many early islands in the South Pacific.

There was enough space on that flat area to house 1,200 Marines in tents. It was soon to grow and grow and grow. This was our home for the entire one year on the base, and was called Tent Camp #1. There was also Tent Camp #2.

My future residence had already been chosen for me, and I was glad for this. I became part of Headquarters Company, 2nd Battalion, 28th Marine Regiment, 5th Division. Up to this point, we had the 1st Division, 2nd, 3rd, 4th, and we were the 5th. My unit, Headquarters Co., 2nd Battalion, would soon become emblazed in the worst battle of the Marine Corps' history on the small island of Iwo Jima, but we didn't know it then. My primary spec. number was for flamethrower operator. I don't remember the exact numbers of this unit because it was changed. The job, however, did not change. Most of my schooling in the nomenclature and operation of this creature was at night. Here I learned early on how dangerous it could be for the enemy. To turn that equipment toward the enemy and hear his screams as he is dying is something that remains with you all your life. It has certainly remained with me. You never forget it.

A Marine flamethrower operator moves forward to assault a Japanese pillbox on Motoyama Airfield

At the time, to my knowledge, the men who used flamethrowers were handpicked by Col. Chandler Johnson, our Battalion leader. I don't know why I was in the group of eight, but I accepted the responsibility. The danger of lugging a flamethrower will be mentioned in the Iwo Jima segment.

In each Battalion area, they had erected a Quonset hut, and this was our galley (kitchen area). Everything else was housed in tents. My secondary spec. number was 060, which was cook. Over the next two days, I was to meet and unite with the five other cooks with whom I was to become so very close. They were Luther Vaughan, Pop Jimerson, and Charles Harris, who were all killed on Iwo Jimo; and Wylie Donovan, Bill Hummell and myself who were all injured on Iwo Jima, but survived.

Our galley force
Top row left to right: L. R. Vaughan from Virginia, "Pop" Jimerson from Texas, Charles "Joe" Harris from Texas.
Bottom row left to right: Wylie V. Donovan from St. Louis, W. N. (Bill) Hummell from Ohio, and me, M. Frank Walker from Seymour, Indiana

With the help of a Second Lieutenant who should have been with the Boy Scouts back home, we chose up sides. Vaughan, Jimerson, and Harris would be one watch. Donovan, Hummell and I would be the other watch. But as time progressed and who wanted to go on liberty, our make-up changed from day to day. It always seemed that Hummell and I were together.

All six of us had some previous experience with food preparation, but knew nothing about preparing large quantities. We did have a manual which became our bible. Without that book, we would have been a disaster. Only Jimerson, who had been in the Old Corps, had been through baker's school. He had survived Guadalcanal and was about four years older than the rest of us; therefore, he became known to us as Pop. He was 23. We were 18!

Through time we discovered that because we were the cooks, we were in charge of everything that happened in the galley and the mess tent. Boy, what a relief! We were finally able to tell someone else what to do and where to go, a role we happily and skillfully assumed!

We also learned that on our days off, we had to undergo the same training that the rest of the troops did. In other words, first we were Marines, fully trained to kill, and then our secondary jobs were what we did otherwise. Even the Marines who guard the President of the United States have to go through the exact training every year as their counterparts in the field. This is what makes a Marine a Marine.

Within two to three weeks, we were feeding around 1,000 hungry men who constantly complained, but ate like it was going to be their last meal. All six of us cooks began to accept the challenge, and I'm sure the quality of the food reflected that. It became a priority with us and we took pride in it. Yes, it was hard. We were soon working twice as long in a day's time as our counterparts. After putting in a full day of work, I went through Combat Intelligence School at night. Yes, it was difficult, but we all felt this was our crucible!

The challenges of training in the Marine Corps today are no different than what we did all those years ago. It takes a very special person to do it. There is no place for a goof-off. The Marine Corps is for men, not boys. Is it any wonder that all of us are a proud bunch? "Once a Marine, always a Marine" is as true today as it was yesterday. It has been this way since 1775 and it will continue to be.

Ever since 1774, the Corps has always been a force that landed by water. Hence, every Marine must be able to swim, and at times under adverse conditions. Early on, the Marine Corps had erected scaffolding above the water of a pool below, which consisted of three levels: a 20-foot level, a 30-foot level, and a 40-foot level. Everyone had to jump from the 20-foot level; however, the 30 and 40-foot levels were optional. I chose the 30-foot.

The water in the pool had a coating of oil and diesel fuel that had been set on fire. The instructor on top had told us in no uncertain terms that we were to place one hand over our nose and eyes, and the other hand over our testicles before jumping off the scaffolding. There would be someone below to help us get out. Oh boy, I'll never forget that trip down to the water and my body separating the fire on the water. This jump went into the record books.

Incidentally, a friend of mine, Willard Winkley from Shelbyville, Indiana, was on the USS Bismarck Sea, an escort carrier that was hit on February 21, 1945, about 12 miles off Iwo Jima and was sunk. Willard was in the water about 3½ hours before being rescued. The ship had a crew of 800 with 321 losing their lives. Willard had to jump under the exact conditions as I have just described. He went on to complete 21½ years in the Navy. Yes, war is hell; there is no glory in war!

Scaling a 14-foot board wall with a full combat pack on your back, along with your M-1 rifle, requires every bit of strength you can dig up. If you fail, you will fall hard in a pit of dirt, only to try again. And as you get to the top, one last grunt and you throw your leg over the top - you have made it. Every minor success gives you a sense of confidence and pride. This is called the Marine Corps.

Have you ever done a 20-mile forced march with combat gear and a canteen of water bouncing on your hip? It takes a full day and full night with only minor stops. This is part of the crucible that made us what we were, and for most of us, what we are today. It is called determination.

Camp Pendleton had its own firing range, and we had to qualify every year. We had this twit from Minnesota who thought he was God's gift to every woman and to the U.S. Marine Corps. As he would come through our chow line, we actually found everything we could to make his life miserable. The last day of qualifying, there were just a few us because of our conflicting schedules. Vaughan and I were in the "pit" marking targets. We knew when #1 Twit was coming up to fire. Vaughan had five-finger discounted a paper target. For those who might not know, the shooter at 500 yards would fire, making a hole in the paper. Then we would mark it with a wooden plate and send it up so they at the shooter's line would see. We had made holes where the bullet should have been. Never once did we give him a bull'seye. In fact, they were completely off mark. We learned that the instructor was so aggravated that he failed him; and that, along with some of his other antics, caused the instructor to make him go through boot camp all over again. We never saw #1 Twit again. Has my conscience ever bothered me on this? No. None of us would ever want this screwball beside us on Iwo Jima.

I remember another character of the same caliber who yelled as he was landing on Iwo Jima, "I'm not going to stay here very long!" Five minutes later he held up his hand, which was a no-no, and pulled back a stump. He lost his hand and was evacuated. Thank God we didn't have many like him! Our very lives depended on that Marine beside us.

It is true that the officers-in-charge, except the petty 2nd Lieutenants, treated us with respect. They knew our hearts were in what we were doing. The six of us cooks in our 2nd Battalion did become excellent cooks. If we didn't have exactly what we wanted for a good menu, we would take our galley jeep and five-finger discount our supply from one of the other units. We could never depend on the 2nd Lieutenants. They were always men who had just graduated out of Officer's Candidate School and no other slot could be found for them. Our Commander, Lt. Col. Chandler Johnson, despised every one of them, even though he had come up through the ranks and had been one of them himself.

Cooking in the field over a full week bivouac is an experience. We had several star burners that were butane fired, and they would either blow up or not work at all. Several stockpots were always in demand. Skillets were nothing more than sheets of steel which we shined. Water was carried in large canisters. Coffee was made in a 55-gallon drum cut down to size. We would boil the coffee grounds and then add cold water to make the grounds settle to the bottom (if we were lucky). Egg shells were generally added to increase the calcium in the coffee drinker's food diet. (It works!)

Making pancakes for 950 men early in the morning with the star burners sitting on the ground is not easy, even for those of us who were dedicated. The troops, of course, had their own mess kits and washed them in another 55-gallon drum. Sound interesting? I could write a book on cooking for the Marine Corps in the field.

So many of the troops were jealous of us because we had open gate liberty, which meant we were not required to "fall out" with them. They never understood that we worked twice the hours they did. They also felt our Battalion Commander might have been a little partial because he was a chow hound.

Many were the times that one of us would open up the galley for him and he would converse with us. To the ordinary eye, he would sound rough, but when you got to know him, you would notice that twinkle in his eye. He fully understood that we six were giving our "last full measure." But the troops never knew this. It was a sad day for us six when on D+10 on Iwo Jima, as he was pushing forward, a screaming Betty from the Nips found its target and Lt. Col. Johnson was hit and killed instantly, his body blown in a thousand pieces. These things you never forget. He was a leader, whereas his counterparts were, for the most part, back on the beach out of immediate danger (but not always).

Training was crucial. All of us became proficient in judo. We learned how to right parry, left parry, left jab, and right jab with our weapons and bayonets. It so happened on Iwo Jima that this method had to be used on many occasions. It is not a casual affair to kill another human being with a bayonet. But the truth is, in war young men die, and all of Washington cannot change this, even though they sometimes downplay the ferocity and ugliness of battle. It is kill or be killed!

Gradually the tents on Tent Camp #1 gave in to Quonset huts which were much more palatable to live in. So life did change. Our PX (post exchange) was about ten miles from the camp and this is where we could buy a coke, a beer, shaving gear, postage stamps, writing material, a newspaper (if you were lucky), and felt more like normal people. Even just to sit and watch other people became a pastime. A platform had been built on a slope and an entertainer from the states was always a welcome sight. Such names as Bob Hope, Jerry Colonna, Zazu Pitts, Francis Langford were there at different times. This was always a big night out for all of us as we sat on the ground and watched and listened and laughed. Bob Crosby (Bing's brother) was a captain in the Special Services Section of our Division and was quite influential in bringing in fresh talent.

Within weeks, our living and training area was undergoing change. The area that had been only tents soon became something more permanent as Quonset huts and even brick buildings began to spring up. America was at war and it became more and more evident. Marine Corps buses began to take us to the PX, to the theater, or to church. It was a beehive of activity.

At this point, we (the Regiment) adopted the cutest lion cub. We named him Roscoe and he had a terrific personality, but woe to the person who tried to tease him. That person would have had all of us on him within ten seconds, plus the Dog Platoon, who were charged with his well-being. Oh yes, we had dogs on Iwo Jima and I'm quite certain they saved the lives of many Marines by sniffing out the enemy. Roscoe's home later became the San Diego Zoo as we went overseas to train and fight on Iwo Jima. It was truly a sorry day when we had to give him up.

He was one of us. We had elevated his rank to Sergeant, and he thoroughly enjoyed his new status. He told us so!

It seemed as though there was never-ending trainings or exercises in our schedule. One maneuver was the disembarkation of troops and equipment off the "mother ship", down cargo nets, then onto a landing craft. The concept of the maneuver would seem simple. Wrong! To work yourself down the "Jacob's ladder" onto a bouncing Higgins boat with all your gear fastened to you requires every bit of stamina you can muster, especially when the man above you is stepping on your hands and the butt of his rifle is knocking you senseless. If you lose your grip, down you go.

In war time, during this descent, you are not given a second chance. You become a casualty and your life is snatched away from you.

How we were to recall and appreciate these exercises at San Clemente Island off the coast of California as we were trying to land for the invasion of Iwo Jima! On February 19, 1945, the seas of Iwo Jima were especially turbulent. The Higgins boat could easily be six feet away from the landing net, and if you dropped down for whatever reason, you would be dropping into oblivion. You had to time yourself at the exact moment, which was impossible with the one on top you breaking your grip on the rope with his weight. But gradually, we became proficient, if not expert, in our training.

This part of our training was so very realistic, and served us well in preparing for the real thing later on at Iwo Jima. For the person who has never gone through it, I will try to draw you a visual picture. You're crawling forward in the sand with your entire body hugging the ground. Your grenades are dragging through the soil, your cartridge belt is full of grit, you're using your rifle to help propel yourself forward, and all the time that rifle is becoming more and more inoperable. Your combat pack on your back (if you have one) has loosened up to where it is just hanging. Your eyes are full of dirt, your stomach is queasy, you want to raise your head to see where you're going, you're afraid to raise your elbows because the real bullets are whining just inches above your head, and you begin to realize if you don't keep your wits about you, you will go into extinction. All of this is as it was on Iwo Jima at 9:00 on February 19th, 1945. Was this kind of training necessary at Camp Pendleton? You bet it was!

Every man, regardless of his job, was a part of this heavy training. It made no difference whether you were a cook, a clerk, a supply man, in the band, or laundry rear echelon, you became one fighting man, trained to kill. It became no place for a slacker. In fact, slackers had been weeded out months before. But this is what makes a Marine a Marine. It has been that way since 1776, and it will always be!

Finally, after every man was in superior physical condition, the day of the final parade became closer. Our uniforms were all spiffed up, our equipment was shined and polished, our senior Non-Commissioned Officers and Commissioned Officers were more congenial and we were told they were proud of us. It was on that day, with the Marine Corps' band playing on the parade ground, that a huge black limousine drove up to the reviewing stand. President Franklin Delano Roosevelt was helped out and into his wheelchair. Could we have felt more proud? No. I have often wondered if he, at that moment, knew what was in store for us. The Marine Corps' recruits were his boys.

CHAPTER SEVEN
WAIMEA AND CAMP TARAWA, HAWAII

Corporal Frank Walker in Hawaii

In looking backward to 65 years ago, it would be very hard to find a Marine who did not have fond memories of Waimea, Hawaii, and Kohala, and what was to become Camp Tarawa. The people in this mountain region of Hawaii might have looked a little different than the U.S. Marines in green uniforms, but there was an immediate bond between the few out of the Army's 299th Infantry, the Marines from the 2nd Division, and then those of us in the 5th Division as we became their neighbors and friends overnight. The people who lived there were the most genuine and trustworthy people I have ever known. You knew you had a friend in them. Apparently they felt the same emotional well-being with us. The bond is what made our time in their midst so terrific. I suppose it is true that they viewed us as their protectors because these people did feel that Japan would invade their homes after what happened at Pearl Harbor on December 7th, 1941. But there was more to it than just fear. They seemed to love us as we did them.

Shortly after the Battle for Midway in early 1942, elements of the 299th Army Infantry had scraped out a small area atop the volcanic mountains which had been given to them by the directors of Parker Ranch, the oldest and largest working cattle ranch in all of Hawaii and America. The area was short-lived, and soon the survivors of the campaign for Tarawa took over. It was more of a rest area because they (the 2nd Marine Division) were tired, sick and needed a home. The Battle of Tarawa was, up to that point, the bloodiest battle of the war with Japan. And then came the entire 5th Division of the Marines. At this point, it became a beehive of intense activity. Electricity, water, a hospital, USO theaters, 5th Division Headquarters, and roads were installed. Saddle Back Road became a highway instead of a muddy trail. And below, in the canyons, there were Victory Gardens and acres of beans and potatoes. It was beautiful to see.

But to go back just a little, we, the 5th Division, had been told our training at Camp Pendleton was coming to an end and we would have to leave our beloved United States of America. We boarded 6 x 6 trucks and returned down the coast of California to San Diego. Upon entering the city limits of San Diego, we passed under the giant nets that were camouflaging the aircraft factories underneath. Upon leaving this area, we were taken to the waterfront and everything was working exactly as planned.

Unit by unit, as our name was called, we boarded our transport ship and saluted as we were getting onboard. A Navy escort showed us to the billet that had already been assigned to us. A cursory glance showed us our bunks were fastened on chains, either four or five deep, with only about 20 inches from each other. We would take a deep breath in fear that a heavy person on top would squeeze us. Sorry, no room to turn over. Whoever designed that transport must have thought we were all midgets. This was when we came to the full realization that this was indeed war time!

Finally, the next morning, we were all onboard. Motor transports and the Navy had worked all night loading sea bags and tons of equipment. The sun was up as the lines were unleashed and we began to glide out of the harbor. We passed by the North Island Naval Air Station and other landmarks and finally the U.S.A. was barely visible. This leaves you with a lump in your throat as you begin to wonder how many will never live to see that shoreline again. But you never think it might me you. It's always the other person.

So now the ship was loaded and all of us, along with the captain, were completely on our own. Goodbye U.S.A.!! I thought of my family back home. I couldn't tell them what was happening. My entire high school days passed before me and I wondered where my childhood had gone. Would I ever get a glimpse of Pauley's Camp back home again? Would I once more get to walk with Mom, Dad, and Ramona on those five acres we had called home? I had to draw on the inner strength I had developed during those early days, and often found solace in the memories I had of my beloved home. I was now a man, going on 19 years old, whose duty it was to defend my country. I wondered if I was ready. And I thought, "Yes, I'm ready because I love my America!"

After about six days onboard ship, we arrived at the harbor of Hilo on the "big island" of Hawaii. This was truly an experience because of the glamour that has always been associated with the countryside. We had perhaps grown up hearing Hilo Hattie on our radio. And who could forget Don Ho and the beautiful music. May I say, not like the noise we hear today!

After unloading, we were met by dozens of beautiful girls with their sarongs and leis around their necks. What a transfusion this was after going through the training at Camp Pendleton! They burst out in song and dance and what a welcome! I looked at the foliage around me and was dumbstruck by the beauty of Hawaii. Some of us enjoyed coffee and cookies provided by the U.S.O. The Red Cross was also there passing out bathroom essentials and stationary, which we greatly appreciated. All this was fleeting and soon reality set back in.

Some units boarded trucks to go up the mountainside, but my unit climbed on a flatbed sugar cane train. There were about ten flatcars (used for hauling sugar cane) pulled by a very tiny chug-chug of a locomotive. This was on a narrow gauge track about 36" across. By the time we were all loaded, along with our sea-bags and gear, that train began to strain. I can imagine the engine looking at the track, and all of us gung-ho Marines, and it probably said to itself, "I think I can, I think I can!" We crossed over Saddleback Road and up and up we went, over gullies and through farmland. We came to a very deep ravine and crossed over on a bridge. I made the mistake of glancing below. It must have been 2000 yards down and here we were on that track that had been attached to underpinnings that looked like toothpicks! I wondered if this was the end of the road for me. I wasn't quite ready to die yet. The black smoke was coming out of that determined little loco, as if to say, "I've done this before!" That was one long bridge!

Well, it did make it and immediately we started up an extremely intense grade. The black smoke was bellowing from the tiny loco and finally it began to shudder – we could feel it! But thanks to the Marines, who are always ready, they jumped off the back car and spent the next 15 minutes pushing it to help out. That exhausted loco heaved a big thanks and a flat area was just ahead. There were several 6 x 6 trucks awaiting us to take us the rest of the way. In that flat area is where the train backed up and turned around to go back down the hill. I will always wonder what kind of brakes it had! We unloaded and our trusty 6 x 6 Jimmies took us the rest of the way.

When we reached our destination, we looked around and I'm sure each one was wondering, "Where did I go wrong?" The tents that we saw stacked on the ground were old, musty, and badly in need of repair. We could tell what had been a street, albeit muddy, so we began the task of setting ourselves up with no help from others. Oh well, we were Marines, and this was war.

Motor Transport had brought in a Quonset hut overnight which proved to be our galley. Soon we were in business.

Within days, we became the owners of a very complete and modern galley. We had steam vats, huge electric mixers, tables and benches, and a large revolving oven. Leave it to the Marines! We must have five-finger discounted most of it from the Army, but when in need, "finders keepers". It was ours.

One might think because we had undergone such rigorous training at Camp Pendleton that things would ease up. Wrong! The training became even more intense. The only difference was that we knew we were overseas for a purpose and perhaps it was our attitude that changed. Men armed with rifles, BAR's, bayonets, and flamethrowers teamed up with artillery units bearing 37's, 75's, and 105's, all worked together as one fighting unit. We would march down the slope of Mauna Kea to a coastal camp on the water, where we would practice more landing maneuvers. The morale was high and strengthening daily. There was seldom any griping or complaining. All of us knew we were being prepared for something of major significance. We knew not what.

While back in camp, trips to Oahu were scheduled. We were allowed to visit the huge city of Honolulu, and even took a short trip into Pearl Harbor. I was awestruck at the devastation that still existed 1½ years after the unexpected Japanese attack on Pearl Harbor. I began to realize it could happen to our mainland. This was very sobering. And just to the left was Ford Island where so much of our military (Marine Corps and Navy) was based. This area was totally annihilated, blown to smithereens by the enemy! And up further on the right was

Hickam Field, where dozens of planes were on the ground completely destroyed. Buildings had been entirely demolished. The powerful American battleship, the USS Arizona, was lying on its side, along with other vessels. And all of this happened on December 7th, 1941, because we were not prepared to react. We had been lulled into a period of platitude! Our "brass" was waking up from a good night's sleep, President Roosevelt saying it could happen – and it did!

But all of that is another story. We, the U.S. Marine Corps, and certainly our 5th Division were here to readjust the attitude of Japan. Every bit of training went into this premise that it will not happen again. And as you can surely imagine, after seeing all that we had witnessed at Pearl Harbor, our resolve was further deepened and any doubts we had entertained were out the window.

Perhaps this is the reason our training had become more intense. While in camp at Tarawa, we six cooks gave it all we had. The Marine Corps (and people back home) were furnishing us with terrific food. Our battalion was receiving food that most had never been used to, not even back home. In our two shifts, the three of us were trying to outdo the other. Steaks replaced spam. Powdered eggs were replaced by fresh eggs. But we all knew that down the road this would change. We knew why we were there, but no one could imagine the carnage that was coming. The name of Iwo Jima had never been given to us. The planning of the island had been on the drawing boards for a long time; but, of course, we never knew it. Tight security was the law and we knew that, too.

At this point I'll bring into the story a happening that could have had severe consequences.

Headquarters had brought in a new fellow to our unit. Now this guy was dumber than a box of rocks. He had apparently been shifted from one job to another and failed every time. Why they ever thought we could make a cook out of him, I'll never know. We did learn from his record that he was an expert rifleman. In fact, he was even better than expert. He never missed a bullseye, which might explain why they kept him in the Marine Corps. He could hit the behind of a fly at 500 yards every time! But somehow he missed the boat when it came to common sense. To give you an example of this, one day we were going to have split pea soup. I had sent him into the salad room to open six one-gallon cans of peas. After about an hour, Bill Hummell and I went into the room to see how he was negotiating this job. We discovered he was taking a knife and was splitting each pea in two parts. I won't put down on paper the reaction that Bill and I had, but I can tell you that it wasn't pleasant.

We had given him the bottom bunk for sleeping. He had the habit of going to sleep with both arms hanging over the side as if he were dead, and then he would start to snore. If you can imagine a Caterpillar tractor straining and coughing to tear down a building, this was what he sounded like. In no way could the rest of us get any sleep. In an effort to break him

71

of the annoying snoring, we started placing one of his hands in a pan of warm water. In case you don't know, this will cause someone to urinate all over themselves. He would wake up and start cussing. By this time he had stormed around and had the entire Headquarters Co. awake with total melee happening in the Quanset hut. But this one particular time, after going through this routine, he ran out the door carrying his rifle. Everyone was either laughing or cussing and thought this was the end of it. But about 30 seconds later, he fired his M-1 into the hut and followed with two more shots. By this time, the C.Q. had heard the commotion and came running. With the help of two or three, they disarmed him. Where he ever got his live ammo, we never found out. We soon discovered they hauled him off and we never saw him again. Thank goodness! We did not need that kind of person on Iwo Jima with us.

While I'm writing this, I am reminded that just this week in Iraq, an Army Sergeant needed a readjustment and shot and killed five Army men. It can happen, and it does happen. War is not pleasant. In fact, war is horrible.

For most of us in the Marine Corps, we found that sometimes you meet someone and immediately there is a bond made. This was the case of me and Bill Hummell. Bill was from farm country around Chillicothe, Ohio, and I was from farm country in Indiana. Because of this brotherly bond, he saved my life on Iwo Jima, and I have perhaps saved his. In the states, we had always gone on liberty together. We had the same values in life. In other words, he was a true brother in arms.

It so happened that both of us loved ice-cold milk. Even though we were receiving the best of food, it was always powdered milk we were given. Powdered milk is a far cry from the real thing.

On one of our mornings off, we discovered a tiny valley that was down the mountainside from the west. We found that valley with lush foliage and flowers blooming to be the most beautiful place in Hawaii. Early in the morning as the sun was coming up with a slight mist in the air, that place was beyond words to describe. It would be just cool enough to make it an exotic place. In that valley were scattered several houses with large gardens. It truly was a Norman Rockwell picture. Up a short lane, one of the houses had a mailbox and a box for milk delivery at the end of their drive. This one morning as the sun was beginning to break through the trees, we discovered quarts of ice cold milk that had just been delivered. This was unhomogenized milk, the kind where the cream is on top. It's like eating ice cream with tiny bits of ice. Well, to some, they might have the same reaction to an ice-cold beer. To Bill and I the temptation was too great. We stood there and drank a quart apiece. We had some change with us and we dropped it in the box and continued on our journey.

Every other morning, when possible, we would make the mile-long run to the valley down the mountainside. Invariably there was an extra quart of milk in the milk box. We never met our benefactor to thank, but in retrospect, they were probably saying "thank you" to us. Years later, I wanted to find out their name and address and send them some money for what they were doing for us. Sometimes it's the small things that count!

Before we had become modernized, our bathroom was in a small Quonset hut. In the front was open sinks for shaving and separated from this area was a narrow platform with ten holes in it about two feet apart. Underneath was a trough of running water that had a downward grade of about 25%. This was designed to carry the waste down the trough. While shaving, a few (including myself) decided to wad up newspapers, toilet paper and anything that would burn. The object was to place these wads of paper in the front part of the trough and set fire to them, which we did. We exited the shaving area pronto and listened to what we knew was going to happen. The first wad hit the bare bottom of the first Marine, and immediately we witnessed, "Y'all, come forth!" By the time the burning paper floated to the middle of the row, I can imagine it was a solid row of Marines rubbing their behinds and trying to pull up their skivvies. We didn't see this part because by now we were long gone. But for the next two or three days, we kept hearing remarks like, "If I ever find the S.O.B. that did that, I'll kill him!" We had to keep a sober face as they would go through the chow line. End of story. They never found out! (Unless they happen to read this book. Oh boy!!)

If there had been committee grading in the 5th Division, and certainly in our 28th Regiment, they would have to had given us an A+. We were the best trained, the most gung-ho, the most ready with the highest morale in the entire Marine

Corps. We had come there as boys and had grown to men in just two years. We had seen many try it and then disappear because they could not cut it. We were proud Marines, fully trained, and ready for the fight that we knew would come. And so, our days at Camp Tarawa were coming to a close.

We had taken on Motor Transport Battalion, a Seabee Unit (31st Naval Construction), Signal Battalion, Pioneer Battalion (construction, the 471st Amphibian Company – Negroes. Remember the country was not integrated yet.) Oh yes, they were destined to be in as much danger as we, and never received the credit due them. Every technical group became part of our Division. This included the 27th and the 31st Replacement Regiment, which very soon, actually within hours, became integrated into us. We then became a part of the 5th Amphibian Corps which included the 4th Division and the 3rd Division. Never in America had this happened.

We began to break camp in early December of 1944. Some went to Guam, others to Saipan. We were all destined for the same place, but we knew not where. We had completed our battle training and the morale was high. The 5th Division was ready for combat and I'm very sure the 4th and 3rd Divisions were ready, too.

We cooks had a slight glitch, though. We had planned a complete turkey dinner while the rest were breaking camp on Christmas day. Apparently the supply shed at Hilo had turned off the electricity early and by the time we got the turkeys, they were green – no good. We had nothing left but hot dogs and sausage. So that was the Christmas dinner that we served our troops. They grumbled on that one for a week! I'm sure our 2nd Lt., our mess officer, received a good chewing out on that one. We never saw him again!

And now it was off to war.

CHAPTER EIGHT
IWO JIMA

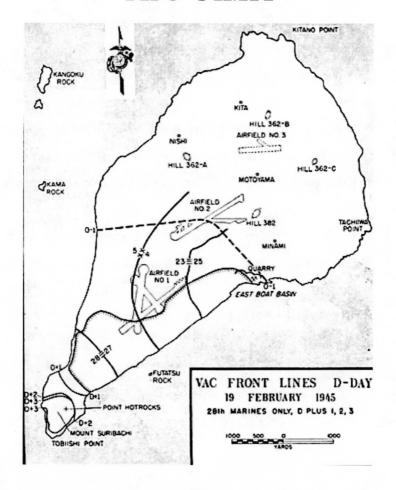

KITANO POINT

KANGOKU
ROCK

KITA

HILL 362-B

AIRFIELD NO. 3

NISHI

HILL 362-A

MOTOYAMA

HILL 362-C

KAMA
ROCK

AIRFIELD
NO. 2

HILL 382

O-1

TACHIIWI
POINT

MINAMI

5

23 ≡ 25

AIRFIELD
NO 1

QUARRY

O-1

EAST BOAT BASIN

28 ≡ 27

O+1

FUTATSU
ROCK

O+2
O+3
O+3

D+1

POINT HOTROCKS

O+2

MOUNT SURIBACHI

TOBIISHI POINT

VAC FRONT LINES D–DAY
19 FEBRUARY 1945
28th MARINES ONLY, D PLUS 1, 2, 3

1000   500   O   1000
YARDS

In collecting my thoughts for this book, I can only relate to Iwo Jima as I experienced it. You will more clearly understand as you continue reading why I kept no notes. As far as the chronology of events, I have relied partly on the information in our 5th Division Green Book, which has become a priceless document to me. I have used the book hundreds of times in locating names of those who were killed and those who were not. It has become invaluable to me as I give presentations on Iwo Jima to hundreds of libraries and schools throughout Indiana.

Memory can be tricky, especially in circumstances as extreme as war; but you may rest assured that there is nothing in this book that is not exactly the way I remember it. It certainly is not my intention to have anything printed in my name that is not factual.

So now, let me start the journey down the hill to Hilo, Hawaii, to where we board ship and begin the journey to Iwo Jima. Of course we didn't know it at this time, but a heavy percentage of these men would never return. These were my friends, my brothers. It's not easy to remember!

We in the 2nd Battalion began to break camp on December 26th, 1944. It was a process that taxed all of us to the limit. We had knapsacks which were to be carried on our backs. Now what sort of things do you pack in a knapsack to take with you into battle? You soon discover that you can't take much more than what you came into this world with, almost nothing. Some might take a Bible, maybe a picture of their parents or girlfriend, or perhaps an address book. But more importantly would have been an extra pair of skivvies, shaving items, toothpaste and brush, extra socks, and your trusty Marine blanket. You soon develop a fatalistic attitude, that whatever will be will be.

So after packing everything else, except the above, into our sea bags, we began to feel the urgency of our actions. The sea bags were hauled away to the Battalion Quartermaster Warehouse.

For the next two days, we six cooks were busy securing our galley. Pots had to be thoroughly cleaned, the floor spotless, refrigeration turned off and food dumped. Our thoughts were, "What the devil? We'll all be back here in a few weeks!" The story has been told of the captain who called three of his charges together and told them, "Now hear up you three. Two of you will not come back!" All three looked at each other and thought, "You poor son of a bitch!" It is true that you never think it will be you! But it so happened that three of our six cooks would never come back and they were killed on the Hell-hole Iwo

Jima. The other three, including myself, were all wounded, but we were still living.

We spent several days encamped on a grassy spot just off the docking area. We looked around but didn't see a single transport that would be taking us to "nowhere." Our area began to become more and more crowded as the 13th Artillery Regiment arrived. Then the Amphibian Tractor Battalion arrived, as did many other units. It soon became evident that the entire 5th Division was on the move. It was in reality quite a sight.

Finally on or about January 14th, 1945, we began to notice more and more ships in the harbor and then the USS Missoula (APA211) came gliding in. That was us! That transport had been so heavily armed that it looked more like a battleship. We wondered where we were going with all those big guns ready to fire. We would soon find out. We boarded ship and began to settle in as that mighty vessel glided around the south end of Hawaii, went to the island of Oahu, and finally weighed anchor at the mouth of Pearl Harbor. Twenty-five percent were given liberty in Honolulu for 24 hours and twenty-five percent the next day. These liberty passes were always given after a two hour unit lecture by some Second Lieutenant on the results of striking up a too-friendly acquaintance with a "lady of the street." Unfortunately, some did not take heed and befell the consequences! Oh well, some will never learn!

Lt. Col. Johnson had volunteered the cooks' services and we began helping out in the ship's galley. Actually, we were happy to do this since it meant good food, all the coffee we wanted, and new friendships. The Navy guys always looked on us in awe and I'm sure we soaked it all up.

Finally, after picking up other elements of our Division, we were ready for the journey on or about January 16th, 1945. Remember, we still didn't know where we were going. We glided out of Pearl Harbor and headed in a westernly direction. The troops onboard ship spent the days doing calisthenics and attending more lectures. We six cooks were exempt from this because our time was spent in the galley every day. The scuttlebutt was running waist deep. Bets were being made as to where we were going to hit and when.

About two days out of Pearl Harbor, we discovered a covey of birds that were following us. From the beginning, we cooks never failed to antagonize some of the troops. That evening we were serving creamed chicken on toast which everyone loved. We passed the word that we had killed those birds and that was what they had eaten instead of their sh-- on shingles. Within a few minutes the ship was already rocking from a high sea and the entire upper decks were lined with gung-ho Marines upchucking into the ocean. We laughed and laughed. Nobody else ever knew the difference. The next morning, after a sleepless night, the troops were pale and tired. We cooks hadn't made any friends, I'm sure. But who needed friends? We had our fun!

Immediately after leaving Pearl Harbor, we began to take on a zig-zag course. We knew that at that point we were in a war zone. We headed for Saipan-Tinian where we were to pick up more troops and supplies. Just off Saipan, we ran into a typhoon. That massive ship, even with its tremendous size and weight, would sink deep into a ravine of water. We thought it would never pull out and then gradually that great vessel was resting on top of the water. The descent with the incline was as much as 50 feet up and down during that storm. Can you imagine trying to cook in a tiny galley with pans flying all around? Nobody ever said the military was going to be easy, did they?

Finally at Saipan, we picked up more armada elements of the 4th Division and from there to the island of Guam, elements of the 3rd Division. I took a short liberty off ship to examine Guam, which had been wrestled from the Japanese just four months before. The results of this battle were very much in evidence even in January and February of 1945.

We had been told about two days out of Hawaii where we were headed – Iwo Jima. Most of us had never heard of this place and we spent a lot of hours looking at maps, some of which didn't even show Iwo Jima. Because of its size, eight square miles, we thought we might be there a short week, then on to Okinawa, which would be our main battle. Even the "brass" hadn't considered the possibility that we could be annihilated and unable to continue.

We became part of a huge armada of ships of every description. We had aircraft carriers, carrier escorts, battle wagons, heavy and light cruisers, such heavily armed transports they resembled

battleships, supply vessels, tankers, LST's, and submarines.....
you name it! There were 880 ships of every description. There
had never been any group this large to form in one convoy prior
to this event. We kept wondering why, if Iwo Jima is so tiny,
did we need all this power. It just didn't make sense.

It so happened that our generals and admirals, along with
President Roosevelt had been arguing this for several months
prior to Roosevelt dying of a stroke. China had never been
our friend and General McArthur wanted to neutralize both
China and Japan completely. When President Truman replaced
our deceased President, the long-standing disagreement finally
came to a head. Truman won out by firing McArthur. These
facts are not generally known, but are true.

Finally some of our generals and President Roosevelt agreed
that we had to hit Japan hard and we needed the airfield on that
tiny island to bring Japan to its knees. No one could estimate
the cost. It seemed to us that it should be fairly easy, but in
reality it turned out to be the very worst battle of the entire
Marine Corps since its inception in 1776. This is how wrong
Washington, D.C. was. But of course, no one could begin to
know the course of history at this point.

There was and still is the discussion as to why, if we had
the atomic bomb, did we need to take Iwo Jima. And then the
subject is always turned around. If Iwo Jima was so important,
then why did we need to use the atomic bomb?

To begin with, the "bomb" had not been tested to the extent
that a decision could have been made. But in my uneducated

opinion, it took the two, the bomb (which was dropped on Hiroshima August 6th, 1945), and the battle of Iwo Jima (February 19th – March 26th, 1945), to force Japan to give up their militaristic attitude and surrender.

Finally, after picking up troops and the myriad of supplies we would need, we were on our way. No one could begin to guess the incomprehensible scene of carnage that was soon take place on that tiny island. The mind is incapable of understanding the bloodshed that runs, the agony of war, the nightmares that the survivors have to this day, unless the reader has been through it.

As I was standing on an upper deck of the Missoula at about daybreak, I gazed out across to the horizon and Mt. Suribachi looked like a solid mass of gray or black in that ocean.

Iwo Jima as seen from the deck of the Missoula

We had already eaten our last meal, which was steak and eggs. The Navy was busy getting ready to launch us Marines over the side. I never understood that last meal. I compared it to a convicted killer who was going to be executed. Would his thoughts be the same as mine and the one standing beside me? What is it like to die? Does it take long? Will anybody remember me? Will anybody know why we are here? Does anybody really care?

For those of us who had been raised in the church, we knew that God does care. But I couldn't help but wonder, "If He cares, why am I looking at this sea of ships? What are they doing? Where is the wrong and where is the right in all of this?"

Suddenly I was thinking backward to my early youth in America's heartland, to my carefree days at Pauley's Camp and dangling a line in the waters of White River. I was thinking of Mom and Dad. Would they ever know what happened? Was I ready for what was coming? I shivered and shook, not really knowing why. I looked all around me and discovered everyone close to me at the rail was quiet. Some had tears. I realized I was not alone in my thoughts. I remembered reading a quote written by Brendan Francis: "Many of our fears are tissue paper thin and a single courageous step would carry us clear through them." How very true those words were then and are now.

It was at that moment I pulled on the strength of character I had been given in my youth and resolved to step forward with courage. And at that moment I became more aware of what was happening all around me.

As I was shaking myself out of these thoughts, almost simultaneously came the order over the intercom, "Prepare to board your landing craft." Bill Hummell and I told each other that we were ready. He grinned and said, "I wish I had another cup of coffee." I smiled back at my buddy and said, "Me, too!" We jumped over the rail and hung on to that Jacob's ladder. Even though we had practiced this maneuver dozens of times, this time was tougher. The seas were swirling and it was a rough ride down that ladder onto our LCVT (landing craft) which was bouncing up and down. You must leave the ladder at the exact moment the landing craft is at its highest peak. Otherwise you would find yourself between the mother ship and your landing craft. Many have lost their lives in this operation. Wiping the salt water spray from my watch, I found I was onboard the landing craft at 0650 hours (ten minutes till seven a.m.) And at this point, I knew there was no turning back. All of us onboard our LCVT were READY!

I noticed that as we were pulling away, we were becoming part of a circle of other craft. This circle became larger as more and more LCVT's, amphibian tractors, etc, joined in. This exercise was to take just about two hours. And each time, as we would swing around, I was looking right into where I was to land – at the foot of Mt. Suribachi. We in Headquarters Co and E Company had been given our marching orders – land and take Suribachi. That hill turned out to be 562 feet high and we had to get to the top. Lt. Schrier from Easy Company was to be our officer-in-charge. We had no way of knowing what was in store for us.

Tracked landing vehicles (LVTs), jam-packed with 4th Marine Division troop approach the Line of Departure at H-hour on D-day. In the center rear can be seen the control vessels which attempted to maintain order in the landing

The island had been heavily bombarded for 76 days prior to this and we thought there could be no person alive on this island. We were right. They, the enemy, were not ON the island. They, we soon discovered, were INSIDE the hill and therefore hidden from our view!

Every ship was firing away with their guns. There was no let up in the noise. It was continual bombardment. Our Marine and Navy Air were blasting that place from the air to where it resembled an entire island being upheaved. Napalm was being fired from the air and the place was in flames. At about ten minutes before nine o-clock, the noise and firing began to subside and as the circle came around to our landing area, those in the 1st wave cut out of the circle and ran full force onto the shore. The waves of men were designed to cut loose every five minutes and at five minutes till nine, I, on my wave (the 2nd), cut loose from the circle. In looking ahead, it seemed as though the 1st wave made it for the most part pretty good because they were on shore. Then as we, in the 2nd wave, were headed for the shore, all hell broke loose. Most of those in the 1st wave were killed and we, right behind them, had no place to go. We became a solid mass of Marines, lying on our stomachs, hoping to crawl forward even one yard.

The bombardment against us was so heavy that we tried to dig a hole deep enough to where the shrapnel wouldn't hit us. We soon realized the hole we were digging was caving in. It was like digging a hole in a wagonload of wheat. It was impossible to move so our bodies would be below the surface of the sand. I raised my head just enough to see that most of the men in front and to the side of me were either dead, dying, or severely wounded and yelling, "Corpsman, help me!" The Corpsmen, of course, were pinned down as we were. And then I realized, "Hey, you're still living!!" It was at this point I began to search deeply within myself for that thing, although very elusive, called courage. And perhaps at that moment the feeling of complete desperation began to leave me. I then drew upon that reserve within me from which I had been trained as a Marine. That is not to say I was not scared. Oh yes, I was scared!! But the "scare" began to turn into a reaction of determination.

At this point, I began to sense what my dad had been through in World War I at Chateau Thierry and Bellow Wood in France in 1918. Thanks, Dad, for your ability to call the shots for me. You prepared me for this as your dad (my grandfather) did in the Civil War. And those before him, including Sir Francis Drake who also struggled to help establish a new colony and country in a young land called America.

In writing this book, I will make no attempt to put in detail where the 2nd Battalion was on a certain day. To begin with, I kept no diary. Who in the world could keep a diary with the enemy shooting at you 24 hours a day, seven days a week for 36 days? I will leave that part of the battle to someone else. My battle was ten feet in front of me! I can only record some of my thoughts and this is the reason that the Battle of Iwo Jima is so very personal. It is not recording the data, it is trying to renew my memory as to the killing that takes place during war.

The killing actually started a few minutes before this. The Higgins boat that carried us in (about 40 men) was hit broadside by a spigot mortar from the "Hill"! At this time, we had no idea what this instrument of the devil was. It was an elongated tube, about 15 feet long, perhaps 30 inches in diameter and contained the largest amount of explosives you can imagine. It was totally inaccurate in its aim. You never knew where it was going. But we were soon to find out. The Japanese who had devised this thing would have to have been insane! That thing would come through the air (you could see it in its course) and you would swear it was not in your path. But invariably it could change its course and hit you –causing complete devastation. We called them "Screaming Bettys" because they would scream a hideous noise as they were coming down. This "thing" is what hit the Higgins boat that I was on. It tore the gate sideways and the Higgins boat capsized onto its side.

I had to jump over the side and dropped my pack, saving my carbine and cartridge belt and my supply of grenades. Incidentally, there were perhaps four or five killed on the landing craft as it received the direct hit and capsized. The entire beach (landing area) was a complete war zone with overturned landing craft, amphibian tanks, jeeps, and artillery, to where it was almost impossible for the Navy to land us. Yes, this was war. Within minutes, the entire shoreline (our landing area) became solid with overturned landing crafts. The heavy artillery became mired down in the volcanic sand. Marines and Navy were dying and all of this was happening in only about one mile in length. In the while, the noise was so deafening that my ears were ringing and there was no way to lessen the "Hell" in my head. Books have been written as to one unit landing and another unit off to their side and how they advanced 50 yards in ten minutes. When I have read these accounts, I want to say "Bull ....!" In reality, men of the 26th or 27th Regiments were being thrown with the rest of us. They might have been designated to land at a certain place, but it did not happen. The Navy had to land us wherever there was a hole to ram into. It must be remembered, the Navy was suffering casualties also. No one was exempt from this "Hell on Earth." Very little has been written about the Navy who brought us in on Iwo Jima, but they deserve the highest honor we can give them. After all, they had no protection, whereas we had our rifles (in most cases).

After swimming and wading ashore from our destroyed LCVT, it was soon apparent we had to navigate terraces that started at the water's edge. These terraces were from six to twelve feet high, depending on where you were. The surface was the same black, volcanic sand that resembled quicksand. We would crawl forward one yard and slide back two. At least that's the way it seemed.

5th Division Marines land on Red and Green Beaches at the foot of Mount Suribachi under heavy fire coming from enemy positions over-looking the black sand terraces. The 28th Marines had not yet wheeled to the left towards Suribachi. *Department or Defense Photo (USMC)*

Our 13th Regiment (Heavy Artillery) was trying to get in place. My very good friend, George Cattelona, from Raleigh, North Carolina, was a member of this team. Because there was not a firm base to set their 105 mm's on, the projectile they were firing was only inches above us as we were trying to get over the terraces. He has often wondered how many of us in the 2nd Battalion were erroneously hit as they fired that unstable 105 mm. To this day it is one of the nightmares George continues to endure.

As I was inching over the first terrace, I began to slither forward using my legs and hips as leverage. The terrain was heaps of black sand caused from the spigot mortars being fired at us and I inadvertently pushed myself over a dead Marine who was partially covered. I looked at his face and recognized him as one who went through my chow line every day before this. This experience was to haunt me every day from D-Day until the 36th day. And after 64 years, it still haunts me. It's something a person never forgets, as you can imagine.

There is an indelible mark that seers your brain and doesn't let you forget what you have seen. And you make a connection between that Marine who is now dead and think, "Here is one of God's children." You wonder why, and yet you know in war it's either to kill or be killed. As I write this, we all know that WWII was necessary, but we as a nation must start asking ourselves why we have to "build nations" and kill, kill, kill? That question mark still stands in the year of 2010.

Gradually, by D + 2, we in the 2nd Battalion had reached the foothill of the now famous Mt. Suribachi. Flamethrowers had been shoved forward and I grabbed one, only to discover that it was not operable. Finally I got one that was working, and I dragged it all the way up Suribachi. The first few hours, as we started up, were so very dangerous; but as we gained altitude, we soon discovered that the Japanese were mostly at lower elevations and they were the ones who had caused us so much damage. By this time, the roughly 1,200 from our unit who had gotten on the beach had been reduced to 300, either by death or evacuation. Our senior NCO and officers were gone, and for the most part we were on our own. At one point, I discovered that the person directing us was a Private who found himself in front. Rank did not have any place on Iwo Jima while under attack!

In talking to Al Nelson and Leighton Whilhite, two members of our 5th Tank Battalion, they relate how they were confined to their tank because of the heavy fire coming from Suribachi. Their tanks became useless in that sand.

My memory goes back to one of these tanks that was sliding sideways up the third terrace. The track on the tank dug in and chewed up a Marine just underneath the surface. I was perhaps three feet from that scene. The blood and body fluids sprayed onto me and I carried that on my clothes for the remainder of the 36 days.

Tell me, how do you blot this from your memory? How can we dismiss those things that happened from our minds? They will forever be a part of our memory process, try as we may to forget.

Finally on the fourth day, we secured and found ourselves on top of that old volcano called Mt. Suribachi. I was one of about 45 who got to the top. Most were from Easy Company, and the rest of the group was from my group, Headquarters Co. Achieving this had taken a toll on us, burning out every opening we could find, blasting our way up with grenades. But the closer we got to the top, the easier it became.

I remember looking north to Kitano Point (we didn't know its name until later) and wondering, "If we've suffered this many casualties in this short distance, what will the rest of this battle be like?" All of the 4th Division had landed and were attempting to take Motoyama Airfield #1. The 3rd Division had landed (2nd Regiment) and both were suffering severe casualties. According to the "brass" estimates, we should have been walking off this stinking hole by now. How wrong they were!

History books record the two flag raisings, and I will make no attempt to discredit any of the data that came out of that incident. I can only relate the happenings as they affected me. I assure you, the reader, that no one in our group was seeking accolades at this time. We were still shaking in disbelief that we had survived, because looking down the hillside and onto the foothill and landing areas, we could all see our friends who lay dead or dying. We had attained the top and were still living.

Someone had a tiny flag with him, perhaps in his hip pocket. Possibly more out of jest than any overt action, three or four tied this tiny flag onto a bent pipe and stuck it in between rocks. When Lt. Col Johnson saw this from below, he sent our runner, Rene Gagnon, up the hill to replace the first flag with one a lot larger that had been on our flagship. He told Rene to tell Lt. Schrier to send the small flag back down – that he wanted it for a souvenir.

Marines under fire passing the flag up Mt. Suribachi for the first flag raising

When this was accomplished, as most of us were looking down into the enormous hole on the top of the volcano, the six men that the entire world has heard about wired the large flag onto a long pipe, wedged it in between two rocks, and raised the flag.

Immediately there arose a tremendous uproar from below and out in the ocean. Our mighty ships cut loose with their thunderous guns, blasting their fog horns at full volume, and a huge celebration erupted. Those of us up on the hill just stood there wondering what all the commotion was about. We were probably somewhat numb, still wading through the blood of our fallen comrades. In our minds we had just completed our job, one that we had been trained to do. Nothing more, nothing less.

In the meantime, Joe Rosenthal, a reporter and photographer from the Associated Press had climbed the hill along with Gagnon and Marine Sergeant Lewis Lowery, to photograph and record this scene. Joe had been advised by a reporter at the bottom of the hill, "Joe, don't attempt to get up there. There's more hell up there than Hell itself." But Joe Rosenthal did it anyway and recorded those two flag raisings. He took another picture, which was posed, of about 25-30 of us at the base of our flag. I am in that picture, the third man on the left side of the flagpole, the one with the raised rifle.

The posed picture at Iwo Jima taken by Joe Rosenthal. Frank Walker is the third man on the left side of the flagpole.

Joe went down the hill to find a craft to take him away so he could send those images on his film to Guam, and therefore on to the Associated Press. He later said that he expected his gung-ho picture, the one of our group standing under the large flag, to be the one to be sent out by the press. But instead, the second flag raising became the one that the entire world has seen and has become the icon in our history.

There was a period of infighting that surrounded this story after the war. Someone always wanted to gain an advantage and notoriety, but this is the summation as I remember the event.

And this is how Joe related the event until he passed away in 2007 at the age of 93. Thanks, Joe, for the memory.

That afternoon, late on the 23rd of February, 1945, we came down the hill, leaving a few men on top. We were to rejoin our unit, or so we thought, on the north side of the mountain.

What we soon discovered was that our unit, the balance of the 2nd Battalion, had been destroyed. We became a tiny band of ragtag Marines without a commander. They had either been killed or evacuated.

From that point on, each day and night was filled with points of contact with a determined enemy. Blockhouse after blockhouse contained Japanese soldiers determined to kill us. Of course, we were just as determined. I had gone through as many as ten carbines, five or six M1's, and several flamethrowers that were out of commission. The grit had caused our equipment, tanks and artillery to become useless.

Because our 2nd Battalion was in complete disarray with so many already killed, we soon began acting as guerillas, each one searching the spot from where the firings were coming. Apparently Col. Johnson realized this and immediately came up to lead us. Within a few hours of his arrival, groups of replacements came. These were kids, many who had come directly from Parris Island Boot Camp. They were scared, timid, and hadn't received the training that we had. When Col. Johnson discovered what he had been sent, I am sure he cut loose with venom in his voice (which he could sure do!)

We were under extremely intense fire from the northern corner of Suribachi, an area where our artillery couldn't produce damage to the Japanese. We had burnt out every crevice that we could find and yet they would open up on us from some other hole. We spent four days in this area, which was on the west side of the island, between the coast and parallel with Airfield #1. We began to notice men from the 1st and 3rd Battalions moving in to help us. Along with the help of the other battalions, more and more supplies were being shoved forward. We had spent most of our ammo, and I had long ago ditched the flamethrower because of no fuel to replenish it. Very few of us had seen K or C-ration for days, and we were all hungry. But as Col. Johnson began to direct traffic, new supplies and rations began to show up and we could breathe a new spirit within us.

Lt. Col. Chandler Johnson was a born leader. He could be very rough and yet, under this façade, those of us who knew him knew he was a kind, considerate Marine who cared about everyone beneath his command. He had come up through the ranks and had this aura about him that compelled others to follow him wherever he led. This was the Col. Johnson we knew.

To give you an insight into Col. Johnson's personality, I'll take you back to the training area at Camp Tarawa in Hawaii. Our battalion was on a 12 mile hike down a hill onto the coastline through very rough terrain. The idea was to have our packs contain everything we would carry into combat and then board ship on the coast. But we, being cooks, were a little too independent. Instead of the "necessities", we included in our packs boxes of crackers, rolls of salami, and even mayonnaise.

While on a 15 minute break, resting under a palm tree and swatting gnats, we were enjoying the fruits of our deception. But here came Col. Johnson. He was upon us before we could hide our contraband and it was too late to swallow the salami in our mouths. He saw us, walked a few feet and turned around. All six of us said, "Oh Sh..!" We thought we had really had it. Instead, he paused, stood there with that twinkle in his eyes, and said, "Cut me off a few slices and I'll pick them up in a few minutes." This was Col. Johnson, a tremendous man who had at one time said to me, "Walker, I'm going to make a flamethrower out of you." How could I not love this guy who I knew was a true Marine?

As I mentioned before, we, the 2nd Battalion, had been on the island about eight days and had suffered severe casualties and deaths to where we were becoming ineffective. We had been drained of all our strength, had very little to eat, no rest, and battle fatigue had truly set in; and all we could see in front of us, on each side, and in the rear was death and more death. None of us, I'm sure, at this point understood the expert labyrinth of caves and tunnels that the enemy had built underground. We would close up one opening, only to discover deadly fire was coming at us from another elevation. Someone in our group discovered a 1,000 foot tunnel with seven different openings at the side and rear. In fact, some of these openings went clear up to the top of Suribachi. The back of the hill (the northwest corner) was so much worse than the east side, and at the same time heavy fire was coming from Nishi Ridge (to our right) and Hill 362A. We were able to get a few Sherman tanks into the area, but most of them had become disabled.

As I said, Col. Johnson was pulling all of us together to gain control of this area. On March 9th, in mid-afternoon, we heard and witnessed three "screaming Bettys" right over us which landed and exploded precisely where Chandler Johnson was attempting to set up his command post for the area. He was killed instantly, his body in a thousand parts. It only took minutes for us to learn the full impact. Some yahoo on the east beach later tried to say it was from our own friendly fire, but we knew differently. We were there. We heard those mortars. We saw them. They could have been meant for us; but instead, our leader who had brought us through all of our training and was now pulling his battle-weary troops back together, was blown to bits. Of all the death, body parts, blood and carnage around us, this loss proved to be probably the hardest for most of us to take. But in the meantime, bitter fighting was going on from Airfield #1.

Major Pearce took over our tired unit and finally was evacuated. Private First Class Woznick then took over because he found himself in front. Woznick was a personal friend of mine, having been on liberty together in the States. We soon learned that 60 officers in our Division had been killed, and scores were evacuated because of injury. At this point on Iwo Jima, I began to lose track of time. I had lost my watch early on and days and nights ran into each other. For the next several days, we were trying desperately to find the openings in the rock from which the enemy fire was coming. It seemed as though every square foot of that miserable island had to be searched. If we missed a hole, it was certain death.

Somewhere between Hills 361A and 362B on the island, our artillery had broken in the slabs of rock to where it formed a narrow corridor in between. About 30 of us from different units found ourselves under heavy fire from the rear and both sides. We could see beyond there two slabs of rock and a drop-down (or hole) about six feet. We felt if we could get down there, we could get help from our artillery. We formed a line very rapidly as the rear of the group was being hit.

The first man ran and got through. By this time, the Japs had us in their sights. The second man ran and was killed instantly. The third man got through. The fourth man was killed and we pulled him aside. The fifth man got through, and I was number six. I was following the routine of this sniper and I knew I would be killed. I took a deep breath and perhaps uttered "God, be with me!" I ran, he fired and missed me, and here I am today. I have asked myself so many times over these 64 years why, why did that sniper miss me? Was it because God chose me to carry the story of death in war to another generation? I do not know. But I do know that war should not be a part of partisan politics as it has been in today's society.

There was a particular blockhouse (enemy's fort) that has remained in my memory all of these 64 years. It was huge, about six feet square, covered by dirt and rock, but our artillery had opened up the face of it just enough for it to be seen. A tiny piece of canvas kept flapping in the breeze as it covered the aperture. I crawled up with our BAR man covering me, stuck the nozzle of my flamethrower in the hole and pulled the trigger. I must have caught him full blast. There was a hideous scream as the intense heat burnt his body in an instant. To this day I can still hear that ghastly cry. The screams of war will never leave me, and I wonder if the people of America who have never been in severe combat can ever fully comprehend this. It perhaps becomes only words. But to those of us who experienced it, it becomes a part of life until we die. I have read somewhere that in war there are two rules: #1.) Young men die. #2.) All of Washington cannot change rule #1.

Every day and night for 36 days proved to be another day of death for so many. I did not keep notes, as only a few did. Even though they were under continual fire, the Navy Corpsmen did keep notes, mostly for the benefit of the Navy doctors on shore (many of whom were also being killed.)

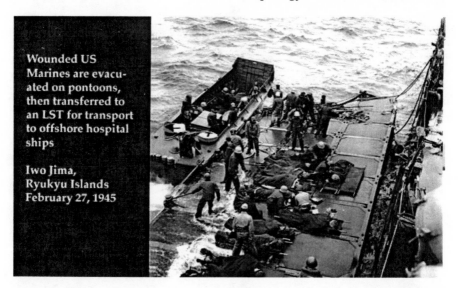

Wounded US Marines are evacuated on pontoons, then transferred to an LST for transport to offshore hospital ships

Iwo Jima, Ryukyu Islands February 27, 1945

There are many times that caught me off guard and caused me to vomit in that black sand which had become purple from the blood of our Marines.

One I remember particularly was on the beach as we were trying to gain a tiny foothold, I was digging in the sand for a pit. I pulled up a Marine's leg, attached to nothing. Tom Nichols, from Clarksville, Tennessee, at the same time was tugging on something rubbery about four feet ahead of me. What he pulled up was several feet of a Marine's intestines. The two of us surmised that it was the same Marine. No other body parts were found.

Iwo is the Japanese word for sulfur, and most of the island was underlain with sulfur pits. For those who do not know, sulfur smells like rotten eggs or worse. From the first moment on Iwo Jima, this odor permeated our lungs, a condition we had to endure until we left. The taste, however, never left. Add to this that it became a frequent occurrence to hear a noise like letting the air out of a bicycle tire, loud at first, then gradually becoming softer, until it stopped. We discovered this eerie sound was a dead soldier who had laid on top of a sulfur pit for days until his body became bloated and was bursting. This discovery, along with the stench of the sulfur, caused our bodies to twist in agony and vomit. You may wonder if this is true. Talk to any Marine who lived through it. Yes, it's true! Very true. This is perhaps why some veterans will not talk about it. But all of this happened on Iwo Jima in February and March of 1945, and there are those in today's society who think there is glory in war!!

For you politicians or anyone who thinks that war is glorious or something to be celebrated, let me ask you a few questions. Have you seen war firsthand? Have you smelled death and dying? Have you tasted the blood of your fallen comrade, lying by your side writhing in pain, pleading for your help – help you had no way to give? Do you think you could stand to watch the sheer terror in your buddy's eyes as he draws his last breath? How about looking at the bloodied and tear-stained face of an injured Marine as your mind flashes back to his youthful grin just weeks before when he came through your chow line? Ever seen your fearless commander's arms and legs blown off like toys? How about shooting into the hideout of the enemy, another human being, someone's beloved son or husband, father or brother who is doing what he has to do for his country, and hearing him shriek in pain and fear and death – ever done that? God help us, I hope you haven't and that you never have to.

And how many of the very politicians who have ordered our country to war have had to go knock on the door of the young fallen warrior's mom and dad and explain that the footfall they were so eager to hear once again would never come? Write it down..... I, Frank Walker, am anti-war, except when every effort has been taken to avert it and it has become absolutely unavoidable! I live every day of my life remembering those horrendous events on Iwo Jima, the playground of the Devil himself. Try as I may to forget, those memories find their way back to the forefront of my mind and haunt me like it all happened yesterday.

In my battalion, the 2nd, out of 1,680 men who landed on Iwo Jima, including our replacements, 1,571 had been killed or evacuated. Only 91 of us got off the island either with or without help. In my company (Headquarters Co.), 120 had landed and 12 of us got out. In Easy Company, 264 had landed with only 27 left. Is it any wonder that we can say it was truly a blood bath and death? Is it any wonder that we veterans are anti-war? I'll let you, the reader, answer that.

With his buddies holding the four corners of the National Colors, the last rites for a fallen Marine are offered by the chaplain at a temporary gravesite in Iwo Jima's black sand. Chaplains of all religious persuasions heroically ministered to all Marines and Corpsmen throughout the thick of the fighting at their own risk.

At the entrance to the 5th Division Cemetery on Iwo Jima, they had erected a sign which read, "When you go home, tell them for us: 'For your tomorrow, we gave our today.'"

The cemetery was being moved to the States even as we were being evacuated to leave the island.

After 24 days of the most bitter battle in the history of the Marine Corps to that date, on March 14th, 1945, the colors were raised once again on Iwo Jima to signify the occupation of the island, although the battle was still raging to the north. The official end of the campaign would not be until 14 days later, on March 26th.

CHAPTER NINE
BACK TO CAMP TARAWA AND ON TO THE OCCUPATION OF JAPAN

So it was back to Guam and finally Camp Tarawa and our nightmare was over. We had departed Iwo Jima on March 26th, 1945, leaving behind our brothers killed on foreign soil. We had left the island with thousands of memories that could never be understood, and probably not even comprehended, by those back home; but we carried with us the pride of knowing we would be Marines for the rest of our lives, and no one could change that. We had upheld every tradition that the Marine Corps had since it was founded in 1776.

It was during this trip back to Camp Tarawa that we learned President Franklin D. Roosevelt had died from a stroke on April 12th, 1945. He had been our Commander-In-Chief and it had an effect on all of us to learn of his death. Harry S. Truman became our new "chief", the 33rd President of the United States, and would prove to be worthy of his position. Incidentally, Adolph Hitler committed suicide on April 30th, 1945, and on May 8th of that year, Germany surrendered.

After arriving back at Hilo, Hawaii, from where we had departed almost four months before, we were trucked up to

Camp Tarawa. That place looked exactly as we had left it. It was almost like they knew we were coming back. Same tents, same everything, including our bunks.

At Hilo, the "brass" had separated everyone as to where we were going. This must have been quite an ordeal, but it went smoothly. While on the beach at Hilo, I had already caught up with Bill Hummell and Wylie Donovan. The others had been killed and would never be a part of this homecoming. The three of us walked into our tent and looked at each other. We had looked in the face of death and had smelled its breath. The three of us hardened Marines let the tears roll down our weather-beaten and weary faces. I was 19 years old. We would never see Luther Vaughan , Charley Harris, or Pop Jimerson again. We three had made it home, the other three had not. There is no way to describe the brotherhood we six had before this, and now there were three. We had gone into the Marine Corps as boys, but now we were men. What a change war can make in a life.

We were all under medical care, but gradually assumed our routine with three replacements who were also veterans, so that bond was sealed. We were back to our six, three-on and three-off schedule.

One day Smitty, our office clerk, called over the intercom and said, "I've got some Purple Heart ribbons for you guys." We looked at each other, knowing full well what the other was thinking, and said in unison, "Smitty, go to Hell!" To each of us, a Purple Heart was meant (or should have been) for that poor soul who lost a limb, or worse. Incidentally, after 64 years, I still feel that way. I say this not to tear down those who have received a Purple Heart; but after witnessing the death and dismemberment of so many of our brothers, this was just the way we felt.

As we were settling into our daily routine, training for the invasion of Japan was very much a part of our lives. Okinawa had been won. Japan was the ultimate goal.

We cooks, with our primary spec. numbers, were expected to help train the replacements who had been shipped in to us. We found out the "boots" regarded us as some kind of gods and would look at us with awe. They had learned of the Hell-Hole called Iwo Jima. It was as if we survivors were like Gunnery Sergeant John Basilone, who was the hero from Guadalcanal days.

We cooks always had open-gate liberty because of our irregular hours, so for the rest of the spring and summer, life for us was a breeze. Taking time off to run over to Hilo, Honokaa, and Kona, along with playing baseball, was a complete diversion of what we had been through. Occasionally there was a trip to Pearl Harbor and Honolulu which was tremendous for us.

While on base at Camp Tarawa, our training and our thoughts were always on what the Invasion of Japan would be like. We were soon to find out.

Early in the morning of September 22, 1945, we onboard ship looked out onto Kyushu, Japan, into parts of the island that somehow had avoided the war. From where we were, all we could see were magnificent high green mountains. As we pulled in closer, we could then see how disastrous war had been for the Japanese. As I was standing on deck, awaiting orders to prepare for landing, I remember a feeling of being privileged to view the beauty of Japan, and yet within yards I beheld complete devastation caused by our bombing. I wondered why the world couldn't remain this beautiful with its majestic mountains and lush valleys. And I still wonder about this same question. I had no animosity against the people of Japan. I had understood years before that it is the governments who become greedy and bullish that create war. God help us!! It is not the citizens. But in Japan, the people had allowed the government and military to take over their lives. As I write this chapter in this book, I am very cognizant of the fact that even in America we were on the verge of this happening in years following 2001. Scary, isn't it? And yet we have North Korea going in a direction that could evolve into war. Please, America, fall back and take a breather from this idiosyncratic action. There is a better way!!

On August 15th, 1945, Japan had accepted the Allies' terms of surrender. We onboard ship had been thoroughly briefed on what to expect as we landed. Peace agreements had been signed by all parties and the war was over. Or so we hoped. Still, we had to be prepared for the worst, especially in light of what had happened at Iwo Jima. The 26th Regiment (CT26) had landed their units at about 0900 hours. We in CT28 were to follow our designated area at about 1300 hours. Our bodies were ready for combat and we were equipped with combat rifles, grenades, and ammo. We were ready but did not expect retaliation. The entire area for our landing was the slimiest you could describe. It had been and was raining and our legs sank deep into this mud. There was no drainage and the smell was horrific. I wondered how this could be since I had been seeing the beauty of Japan from afar. Our 6 x 6's (from Motor Transport) were churning this mess up and getting stuck. At least we would not be trying to get on the beach through the black sand of Iwo Jima.

As I was sinking down to my knees in this goo, I looked over to my right and standing on a part of the dock were several old men and women and children. They carried no guns, nothing. And here we were thinking we might have opposition! They had never seen an American and were probably dismayed that we were actually human beings, even though we didn't look that way at the moment. They had been taught that we were heathens and looked like devils. They must have realized that if we were devils there was no way we could get out of that mud. Not even the Devil himself could negotiate that mess! I had always had faith in our "brass." But how they had misfigured this episode was more than I could understand. It was comical to see the 2nd Lieutenants who had never been in combat stepping high to keep their shined boots clean, only to fall down in this muck.

There was a communal bathroom off to the left and that dung had sunk into the mess we were wading in, and what a smell that was! This is how we landed with our Combat Team 28, with no pomp and ceremony. This was Sasebo, Japan, just off the pier. As you can imagine, curse words were manufactured here, both aimed at the Japanese, along with our brass onboard ship. Oh well, whoever said that life is fair?

We began to load the 6 x 6 trucks, men and mud, into the open backs. As the trucks were ready to pull out, all six wheels were spinning that stinky sludge back into our faces. It was so deep that the truck's differential was dragging in the mud. I noticed that most of the trucks were headed north; but for whatever reason, the truck I was in headed south. I thought maybe the driver was lost, but he was in charge!

It turned out to be a blessing in disguise because we drove south about 30 miles and began to turn to the left which was going north. All of these roads had been bombed out with no hard surface intact, and were therefore paths of mud. Our road was on the slope of a small mountain, and as we looked out to our right, there was the city of Nagasaki, which had been the recipient of the second atomic bomb dropped by the United States on Japan. This second bomb was smaller than the one that had been dropped on Hiroshima just three days earlier, August 6th, 1945. Even though it was the smaller of the two bombs, fully 2/3 of Nagasaki was destroyed, taking with it approximately 150,000 civilians. As we drove by, there were pockets that were still smoldering. It has been estimated that the temperatures on the two cities could have reached as much as 1 million degrees. If a person would have been on their doorstep, there would not even be a grease spot left where they had stood. The center of the city was completely gone. Even the rocks had been melted. As our gaze went out to the edges of the city, it began to appear more inhabitable.

The experience of seeing the mass ruination nearly five weeks after the atom bomb had been dropped was and is so unbelievable. And there it was for us to see! As I have said previously, the question has often been asked, "If the two bombs were that powerful, then why did we have to take Iwo Jima and Okinawa?" The truth is that it took all those to bring Japan to its knees. Our minds cannot comprehend the extent of destruction from that atomic bomb.

We could only get within 500 to 600 yards of the perimeter of the damage because it was still, even after five or six weeks, just too hot, both from heat as well as chemical reaction. And now, in the year of 2009, we find the entire world in an arms race. Does it make sense?

As our mud-laden 6 x 6 truck advanced toward Fukuoka, we in the back of our trusty vehicle looked at each other. All aboard were covered with mud from being splashed by riding over a rough road. Actually the road had long ago disappeared and was nothing more than a muddy trail. Every two or three miles there were huge craters caused by the bombing that our air patrols had delivered to the Japanese. We wondered what the city of Fukuoka would be like. All of us had already seen too much destruction. We were tired and tired of being tired. None of us knew what it was going to be like to occupy an enemy city. But beyond these personal emotions, we knew we were seasoned Marines and could handle anything that would be thrown at us. Call it as you may, whether it was "Esprit D-Corps", or just plain guts.

Finally we arrived at our destination which was the city of Fukuoka. I ended up spending almost nine months at Fukuoka, long after most of our troops had been discharged and gone home. The "brass" told me that I was essential. I was only a cook, but I guess everyone had to eat. Oh, well.

We had been told by the "brass" that Fukuoka would be our base of operations. We in the 28th Regiment had to tear down and destroy anything and everything that was in any way related to the military. In reality, as we were creeping forward toward the city, we could see evidence that the Japanese still had military capability. We passed an airfield that must have contained at least 2500 parked planes. Some of the planes had become disabled by a typhoon that had swept through a few days before. But with Japan's ingenuity, most of these planes were ready to be used against us. That is the reason I have often declared that it took the taking of Iwo Jima, Okinawa, and finally the atomic bombs on Hiroshima and Nagasaki to deliver the final punch for them to surrender. Before those three happenings, they were not a beaten nation.

So here we were, wondering what Fukuoka was going to be like. My inner thoughts, I'm sure, were that not many

Americans had set foot on the soil of Japan, but here I am. To me, a student of history, I had always felt Japan was a strange and mysterious place with everyone wearing kimonos, bowing, and dealing with little gadgets. And here we were in their land to tear away their customs. Not really, but it did seem so strange to me. And then, gradually I began to view this foreign land as their land, the same way that Indiana would seem foreign and mysterious to them. I knew that war is to kill or be killed, but this was not war. This was the beginning of a new season!

If there were any great degree of animosity that I had for them, it would soon disappear. The war was over and now was the time for rebuilding. Those were my thoughts! The verse in Ecclesiastes 3:1 filled my mind, "To everything there is a season, a time for every purpose under Heaven."

Fukuoka was a huge city, the largest on Kyushu, the southernmost island of Japan. At one time, before so many had fled the city, it was a teeming place where close to 400,000 lived. It lies about 80 miles north of Sasebo where we had landed. Our B-2's had blasted a huge section in the center of the city, but most of it was intact and beautiful, untouched by our bombs. The waterfront was a disaster area and it was amazing to see the Japanese picking up and starting to rebuild their lives. We soon learned that the nation hated Tojo and they were ready to reclaim their lives. At first they distrusted us because the government had told them that we, the Americans, were heathens and were from the devil. This is what government can do to its people. It could even happen in America, under the wrong leadership. This is the reason that our 1st Amendment in the Constitution, which claims freedom of speech and freedom of thought, must be protected. Let us never forget this truth!

We began to witness thousands of Korean nationals who were being mustered out of the Japanese Army. They were going to the railroad station where they would be transported down to Sasebo and then to their homes. These were actually Korean slave laborers who had been forced to fight us, perhaps some who had been on Iwo Jima. History has shown us there were about 2 million of these people in Japan at the end of the war.

Different units of our 28th Regiment had been assigned certain areas of operation. Most of them were to demobilize the air fields and any military installations they found.

We cooks, for the first time in our Marine experience, were told to set up and operate the galley. In other words, we were to cook and nothing else. That sounded simple enough, except we had no food to cook and no place to do it. We three cooks, Donovan, Hummell and myself suddenly received three more cooks, making our complement complete for our battalion.

How the "brass" worked all this out was a complete mystery to us, but we sure weren't asking questions. As I have said, we were tired and tired of being tired. We were taken to the Kyushu Imperial University, and soon learned this was to be our home. About ½ of the buildings had been bombed out.

Ours was pretty much intact except the physics and chemistry department. This is where our galley would be, except for one problem. Rats. Almost immediately a fumigation crew came in and took care of the situation. Waterlines were run to our own water purification system. Crews from our battalion (when not on patrol) began to clean the place up. The Pioneer Batallion was called in and overnight we had tables, chairs, and benches. We were in business except one more problem. No food and nothing to cook it on! Just a minor detail! But someone from upper echelon had this figured out, other than scratching his posterior in his off-hours. From Division Quartermaster came a complete kitchen: pots, pans, stoves, and oven from Hawaii. Most of this was being flown in and together we worked all night to get it set up. New electric lines had been connected and we were in Seventh Heaven! All of this happened within 72 hours of our arrival. Our sea bags arrived and our home was in a classroom, next to our galley. A large portable refrigerator had been brought in and set up and immediately food began to arrive. The next morning, even though it was late, we served sausage gravy and biscuits, thanks to one of our new cooks who had been to baker's school. This was Luther Musselwhite, who became a tremendous friend of mine.

For that first meal in our new home, we had about 250 men. They reacted to us cooks as though we were gods! After all, C & K rations do become quite monotonous after a long period of time! The rest of the battalion was on patrol and we soon learned that meals didn't have to be ready any certain time. It was a different experience for sure.

This was the beginning of the nine months I was to serve in the occupation of Japan. Most of the original battalion had been sent home long before. The reason that I was there that long was because the island of Kyushu and our University building had become the focal point for the Army, Navy, Air Corps, and Marines who were all involved in dismantling the military force of Japan. We cooks became essential for all those coming and going. It turned out that we cooks were feeding someone, in groups of six or six hundred, 24 hours a day in a strange land!

By January of 1946, the Marine Corps became less visible and soon most of the operations around Fukuoka were turned over to the Army. In our Division, over 500 officers had been sent home and over 12,000 grunts had left. But the morale in our galley never wavered. We were treated with respect, regardless of the branch of service. This I will always remember!

We could see daily changes in the life around Fukuoka as demilitarizing was happening. Thousands of Koreans were being sent home, as these men had been conscripted into active service for Japan. They were not much better than slaves and had been completely beaten in spirit. Their entire psyche showed how they had been subjected to sub-human treatment for those years. Even on Iwo Jima, it has been written how many hundred Japanese we had taken as prisoners. In reality, they were Koreans. Also, there were about 3,200 Chinese in Japan who were working no better than slaves. All of these were involved in the exodus leaving for their homeland and villages. All of this was being controlled by our forces and it was quite a job.

Thousands of Japanese aircrafts had to be bull-dozed into an enormous pile and burnt. Most of these could have and would have been used against us if the surrender had not taken place when it did.

Our 27th Reg. patrols discovered a huge dump for ammunitions where 1/5 of the country's ammo for defense had been stored. These piles were either blown up or dumped into the ocean. We cooks would hear of these stories as the men would filter in to sit and rest around cups of coffee. Those were very busy weeks for all of us. It was no wonder that we cooks had to cook – that was our job.

There was one short trip that I took, more for diversion than anything else, except I ended up continually cooking on the trip. They had loaded an LST with Chinese to take back to China who were being held as prisoners upon arrival at a small village on the water's edge. We would be bringing back Japanese who had been held for years in China. These Japanese had really been mistreated. Most were on starvation diets. As we were making the transfer of POW's, there was a group of Chinese that were determined to kill the Japs before we could get them aboard. World War III almost broke out, and all I had was my carbine and very little ammo.

It began to dawn on me the degree of hatred that the two sides had for each other, and to this day, it still exists! That was my only trip to China which lasted maybe four hours.

Life gradually became less severe and we were able to take short trips into town. Black Market was all around and we had to be aware of how badly the Japanese needed money. It was so easy to be suckered into a transaction that was silly. We began to pick up enough of their language to get by, and vice-versa. There were parts of Japan that were absolutely beautiful. Those parts had not been destroyed by our bombs. It greatly resembled southern Indiana to me. Even the climate was similar. Quite often, as my wife Jackie and I will be driving down the highway in Indiana, I see a hilltop, a little valley, or a picturesque stream that is identical to a scene in Japan, and I cannot help but make the comparison.

One day on one of my forays into the city, Bill Hummell and I happened to make an acquaintance with a Japanese man who could speak perfect English without an accent. We soon learned that he had been a tailor in Boston, had gone home for a visit, and was unable to return to America because of the war. He was a naturalized American citizen, but Japanese by birth. This friendship that developed was a no-no from our military, but we did it anyway.

It turned that out he made me and Bill Hummell three silk American-style shirts each. He would take no yen for them. When I left Japan, I had shipped three padlocked sea bags to Mare Island, just outside of San Francisco. From there they were to be shipped to my home shortly thereafter. About two months after my return to Indiana, I received exactly ½ of one sea bag, which contained stuff that was useless, and no shirts. Some eager beaver swabbie at Mare Island had five-finger discounted my prized possessions. How long can you hold a grudge? For a long time!

Gradually Kyushu became more Americanized. Their diet became more palatable, their hygiene healthier, and the people no longer stared at us with skepticism, but instead really began to trust us. They had been taught by their government for so long that we, the Americans, were inhumane, and it did take an effort on our part to dispel this attitude. But gradually, and sooner than you might expect, our ambassadorship began to pay off. Fast forward to our present day relations with Japan and you will see that fair play, decency and forgiveness does pay off, even though it does not happen overnight. It took time to dispel the untruths that their government had told them, even as we Americans began to balance everything that came out of Washington. Let us never forget that just because we are Americans, we are not perfect. We are not!

The tearing down of the Japanese military regime was continuing at breakneck speed. It has been written in our Marine Corps' 5th Division Green Book that the 13th Regiment Marines (our Heavy Artillery Unit) had destroyed about 188,000 pounds of heavy artillery ammo, 25,000 aerial bombs, 400 tons of aircraft parts, 30 tons of signal equipment, 1800 machine guns, 250 torpedoes, 650 tons of torpedo parts, 4500 depth chargers, 83 extra-large guns and on and on. Multiply that by the many units of our Marine Corps Navy and Air Force, and you will have to say that the enemy was surely ready to give up.

The Japanese citizens and military were furious with their Prime Minister Hedeki Tojo. They had been lied to and were completely exhausted both mentally and physically. It took the battle at Iwo Jima (February and March, 1945), the battle of Okinawa (April through June of 1945), and the atomic bombs dropped on Hiroshima (August 6th, 1945) and Nagasaki (August 9th, 1945) to get Tojo to finally say, "I give up." Incidentally, Tojo tried to commit suicide in September of 1945. He was found guilty of war crimes and was hanged in December of 1948.

Before I left Japan, they were already rebuilding the part of the University that had been destroyed. Several years later in St. Petersburg, Florida, I had the occasion to do some work for a Japanese surgeon who had received his medical training at Kyushu Imperial University. At the time that I met him, his record had been written up in the Veteran's Administration journals as being extraordinary. He was part of the V.A. system at that time. We had a chance to compare notes and together discovered that I was cooking in the same building and area where he had received his training. It's a small and ironic world, isn't it? Our lands had fiercely fought each other. Immediately after the Peace Treaty was signed, we went to

Japan to help clean up our mess; and now here the Japanese were in America helping to heal their human targets. Wow.

Well, finally my life in the U.S. Marine Corps was coming to a close and I began the process of being discharged, saying goodbyes, and preparing for the long journey back to my home in Indiana. It had been a struggle. I should have been killed a year before. Yet here I was, turning around to catch one last glimpse of my surviving comrades. The physical journey was roughly 6500 miles. The emotional journey was light years. I wondered what was ahead for me now.

Chapter ten
THE AFTERMATH OF WAR

As I prepare to write about the aftermath of war, my mind is overwhelmed with the enormity of it all. War not only affects the individual soldier, it carries over to his (or her) family for generations. Volumes have been written about the Civil War. And here we are in America fighting the injustices that created the Civil War every day in America in the year 2010. After these 160 years since the Civil War started, have we really learned any lessons? Oh yes, we have televisions, we have computers, BlackBerry's, I-Pods, Twitter, and all of these descriptives that I, at age 84 know so little about. But the description of tearing a man's body apart, or living the rest of his life with no legs, or living an existence in a V.A. hospital, or the effects this calamity called war has had on his or her family, is very seldom mentioned. As a result, so many of the new generations of today grow up and say, "If there are any hardships, let the government take care of it." Nathan Hale said, "I only regret that I have but one life to give for my country." There were men in that era of our history who understood that it requires great sacrifices, sometimes against overwhelming odds, and that America is worth fighting for. And they understood there are devastating results of war.

There are no words in the dictionary to portray the destruction caused by war. Pictures might help our society to understand – at least give it lip service. But war is not just pictures. War is your son or daughter, brother or sister, mother or father waiting on the battlefield to be picked up by the litter bearers with his body in a hundred parts. All life has been snuffed out of his or her body, where only a few moments before he or she was perhaps thinking of being reunited with you, his family. He or she, I am sure had high expectations of what he wanted to do "back home" for the rest of his life. But now those high ideals are gone forever. He or she had hopes that if life came down to this, that his life would be remembered. But in too many cases, his life was buried underneath a stone marker in a cemetery. And to make it worse, the cemetery is now grown up with weeds, all but forgotten.

In the meantime, the remainder of his family might be shopping at the mall for a new I-Pod or Blackberry. In the years following, a younger member of his family might ask of someone in the family, "Who was Uncle George?" And the older member might reply, "Oh, I think he was killed, but I don't know where. Seems like it was someplace in Europe. I've got other things on my mind today. Maybe Grandma can help you. I don't think I ever knew."

The same hypothetical "George", some time before his body erupted in so many pieces, had written a "blank check" made payable to the United States of America for an amount that included his very life. He did it because he loved America. The check was not made out to some self-indulging politician, or even the President. The check was made out to the U.S.A., and was cashed by his very life. He or she understood that freedom does not come cheap. Freedom comes with a very heavy price. It comes from the Honor, the Integrity, the Commitment of the millions of "George's" throughout our history as a nation. And too many times it also means the giving of the Supreme Sacrifice, the complete giving of your very self. A life given for our country should never be forgotten.

If in reading this final chapter, The Aftermath of War, you see America in need and say, "Let George do it!" I would say you have a problem with your attitude. Please ask yourself this: How much do I love my country? I see in America an indifference to our values, which makes those of us who do treasure what we have in freedom want to change things before it is too late.

In the book, "The Light and the Glory," written by Peter Marshall (son of the celebrated Peter Marshall in our U.S. Senate years ago) and co-author David Manuel, this statement is made: "How much longer will God bless America?" Yes, reader, it is time to re-evaluate what America may mean to you. This is my main reason for attempting to write this book. It calls for commitment to the purpose and if we do this, then America can once again become a citadel of light for the rest of the world to see.

What we see in our country and society today is an alarming degree of moral decay. You don't have to be a college professor to know this. And right alongside the decency issue is the complete lack of patriotism. As our country sinks deeper into an abyss of moral rot, the lack of patriotism shows its ugly head. It is up to each one of us, the living, to turn this around. Shall we do it? I will echo the Nathan Hale quote I mentioned in my Introduction, "I only regret that I have but one life to give to my country." The founding fathers knew and understood this. And there are many today who understand this. Look around you and when you see one in uniform, go up and thank him, because he is doing a thankless job.

I have only touched upon our most important commodity, the human life. There are many other parts of the aftermath of war that I will touch upon. America has been through many wars in our history. Just to name a few: the Revolutionary War, the French and Indian War, the Mexican War, the Spanish-American War, the Civil War (which took over 500,000 lives), the incursion at Beirut (which took 250 Marines while they were asleep), World War I and World War II, the Korean War where there was no finality, Vietnam, Desert Storm, and this horrendous mess that our country is embroiled in now, plus many others in between all of these I have mentioned.

No, there is no glory in war. But those of us who have lived it, and are still living, deserve respect for the blank check they and we wrote to the U.S.A. This is all we ask – respect. It starts in the home and schools. I have been in some schools where the day is started over the loud speaker with the entire school repeating the Pledge of Allegiance. Yes, there is a glimmer of hope that will be shining as a light upon a hill if we continue. Patriotism is something to be very proud of, nothing to be ashamed of. And it starts with one, which is you who are reading this. And then we can say, "Yes, it is good to be part of America where all can be free, where we have democracy instead of totalitarianism state, where justice does prevail and fair play can exist." We believe that all women, as well as minorities, should be honored in all things and not denigrated. This can be the New America. I have heard the quote, "Even the sun has spots, but its main purpose is to give off light." (Author unknown.) May we as a nation give off light to the rest of the world, but never try and make ourselves better than they.

Another part of the aftermath of war is the tearing up, the ripping up of the beauty of our world that God has made.

In Japan, I discovered part of the landscape entirely beautiful. It was and had been a picture of beauty. But war had decimated so many areas that it looked pathetic. Most of the islands in the Pacific had been picture-perfect. Even Iwo Jima, that tiny oasis in the Pacific, could have been unusual but for war destroying it. In Europe, the Black Forest of Germany had been a sight to take your breath away. The same way with France, and all the Balkan States. At one time London had resembled a complete disaster area. The only things left standing were the underground bomb shelters, and even the roads to them were destroyed. Yes, America was spared, but what about 9-11. It almost happened right here while we were buying electronic toys at Walmart. Who was minding the house? No one. Have we learned any lessons? I hope so! The aftermath of war is hideous. We can never take our freedoms lightly. Let us begin to make America a shining light upon a hill.

America can be great again, but it starts with each and every one of us individually. Let Washington forget its partisan politics and work for America! We pay them to work for us, but somehow that concept has been turned around. Shall we turn it around and let America be beautiful?

Another element of the aftermath of war is what happens to the veterans who have managed to come away with two legs and two arms? What about his mind - the part of him or her that can never forget what he was a part of? I can give personal testimony to this.

When I came home to Indiana and my hometown after surviving the worst battle in the Marine Corps, Iwo Jima, the friends that I knew before, who had stayed home, wanted to throw me a party. I am sure I looked at them in amazement. There was no way that I could have been a part of a party. I should have been in a V.A. Hospital to regain my civility, to try to work through the bloodshed that kept running through my brain. Even today, after 64 years, there is never a day or night that I do not remember it all as if it happened just yesterday. How can I ever forget and accept it all?

Veterans may say, "Oh, I'm okay." But in too many cases it's nothing more than a cover-up. Oh yes, we have the V.A. to go to, but there, according to recent reports, are approximately 300,000 veterans waiting to be treated. The backlog of men and women waiting to be treated is astounding. This is the reason the suicide rate among veterans is so very alarming. These are the facts, and all of Washington cannot change them. This is called the cruelty of war. There is no glory in war.

In writing and putting this together, it has been an excruciating endeavor. Dragging up the memories of so long ago has ripped me up at times. But I knew when I started that it was something I had to do. If by my doing this there has been one person touched with the knowledge of war, then it has been worth the endeavor. This book is not intended to be a "downer" for anyone. It is meant to be a guide for all of us to build a better America. We, as Americans, have so much for which to be thankful. We all can build upon this precept.

A couple of years ago, just before the upcoming election, the Democrat nominee who was running for a House Seat, appeared at a local nursing home to talk to a few people. I felt I knew why he was there, to garner a few votes from those at the nursing home who were not mentally alert because of their age or illness that had struck them down. After he, with his assistants, had registered a few voters, he was going to speak in the dining room to anyone who would listen. I had gone over to the facility to listen to him, and chose a chair in the rear of the room.

After listening for perhaps 15 minutes on how he was going to change the tenor in Washington, how Social Security needed to be changed, how V.A. needed his help, how Medicare should be changed, how the educational system certainly needed his help – all of these were exemplary endeavors, but I knew that he was the proverbial politician that had more hot air than the air hose at Huck's gas station. So, as he was winding up, I (who perhaps was ready for a fight) stood up and asked a question that could have been answered very simply. I said, "Sir, if elected, what can you do in Washington to help stop the partisan bickering and start bringing a sense of patriotism back to our country?" His face turned beet red, he grabbed his briefcase and shot for the door – followed by his driver. He was out the door without uttering one word, and his driver, as he was passing me, said, "He did serve a hitch in the Armed Service." La-de-da!

Needless to say, I did not vote for him. I left the square blank. In following him for these two years, it is very easy to say that he wanted that job in Washington for the paycheck. And that is the type of person we continue to send to Washington to represent us.

Should we, the voters, start expecting more out of our elected men and women? I believe so. We should demand that they come clean with portraying their ambitions. After all, we – all of us – are paying their salaries. And if they do not meet our criteria as to who we want, do not give them a blank check. It is our duty as voters!

A philosopher once wrote, "We can define the world by the questions we ask." In other words, if we, as a people, become so decadent that we don't ask questions as to why we should vote for a certain politician, if we never take Washington and even our President to task as to why they make certain decisions, if we don't question why our foreign policy in the world is always right (just because it came out of Washington?), if we allow society to run over us without objection, then we have become less than the human being that God intended. By giving up this God-given right, we are creating another Hitler or Tojo, or the many like those two, who in their hearts are selfish to the point that they will try to destroy every free-thinking individual in their path.

A partial answer to this negative thought or endeavor is the heartfelt return to patriotism. We need to re-evaluate what America means to each of us. I pity the person who by his words and actions say, "Let the government do it," or "I'm too busy having a good time." Let that person move on to another country where his very thoughts and actions are governed by a dictatorial regime of government.

Every one of our freedoms have been fought and paid for by many who have died to protect those very freedoms. Freedom does not come cheap. It comes from giving and standing up for what is right. And in to final analysis, it means you and me being willing to give our lives for this decision. Our history is sprinkled with millions who were willing and did this for the country they loved, America. Freedom was not bought, paid for, and sealed by one generation. It is a continuing struggle, a continual challenge for each generation before and after us.

Since no society is 100% perfect, we must learn to take the bad with the good, and diligently work on the ills that make it bad and striving for good in America. Sometimes it is easier to dwell on the bad. Irregardless, we still live in the best country on earth. And even though our country may go through trials, we can rest assured that our flag will still be flying.

Until we as a country start to believe in America, until we begin anew to realize the symbolism of our flag in our lives, until we individually can say, "I will fight for our flag because that flag is America," until we start understanding that we need a new sense of nationalism instead of the old sense of individualism, then we will continue this downward trend into gutter politics.

John Winthrop (1638-1707), a colonial military leader who eventually became governor of Massachusetts, said "We must consider that we shall be as a city upon a hill, the eyes of the people are upon us, so that if we shall deal falsely with our God in this work we have undertaken, and so cause Him to withdraw His present help from us, we shall shame the faces of many of God's worthy servants, and cause their prayers to be turned into curses."

I believe America can once again become John Winthrop's "city upon a hill."

In most cases, ordinary people can do extraordinary things. Case in point, Susan B. Anthony – one person who was unwilling to give up and was willing to buck the establishment. Her efforts brought about women's suffrage in America (the right of women to vote). Patriotism can start with you or me. Sometimes it takes only a spark to start a forest fire. That spark spreads in all directions to where the entire mountainside is on fire. It can happen right here in America. And may that spark be spread by you and me. As the world sees us, that will be their reaction to us. Yes, there is an alternative to war. War should be used only as a last resort and not started because we don't like the other side. America, start thinking!

Yes, our country's history is spotted with things that should not have happened. Case in point: Following Pearl Harbor, our government shoved into internment camps in California 100,000 American citizens who happened to be Japanese by origin. (I happen to be Irish by origin.) These people were the salt of the earth, the best farmers in California. But because they looked a little different from some of us, they became our enemy right here in America.

And right here in Jackson County, Indiana, there is an area not ten miles from where I live now called Sauer's area. These families were also the salt of the earth. The parents migrated to the U.S., and the generations from them became true Americans by birth. These parents had already adapted to our society, but because they were Germans by origin, the F.B.I. watched over them as though they were ready to blow up all of southern Indiana. Their telephones were being tapped, their mail was disrupted, and their lives in general were in chaos.

In my youth, our next door family had three sons and one daughter, all of German descent. Two of the sons went into our Army, one was killed in battle, and the daughter was a nurse in the U.S. Air Force. And yet this family was under constant surveillance because their grandparents had migrated to America from Germany.

Yes, we need to stress the need to return to patriotism and the values that have made America great for so many years.

Thomas Paine, one of our very early patriots, once wrote, "In America we have in our power to begin the world over again." And that early statement by Paine is as true today as it was back then when he uttered those words.

Ronald Reagan said in his farewell address to the nation, "I've spoken of the Shining City all my political life… In my mind it was a tall, proud city built on rocks stronger than oceans, windswept, God-blessed, and teeming with people of all kinds living in harmony and peace; a city with free ports that hummed with commerce and creativity. And if there had to be city walls, the walls had doors and the doors were open to anyone with the will and the heart to get here. That's how I saw it, and see it still."

As I enter my 85th year on this earth, I would like all of the following to take the legacy of America to heart. I would ask them to educate themselves on what has made America what it is today. These names are my family: Pat, Nadine, Michael, Kevin, Tracey, Jackie, Logan, Caleb, Aubrey, Jeffrey, Arnold, Barbara, and Christian. If these 13 names in my own family would renew their lives to the legacy of America, don't you think that one family could make a difference? Then multiply this one family by the millions of families in America and you will have that "city upon a hill" which will be the shining star the world looks up to once again.

On the first meeting I had with the co-author of this book, a young lady who was sitting nearby our table overheard our conversation. It is not very often as we go through life that we meet a person who has that talent and natural ability to sit down and write verse and poetry that comes from the heart. This was my experience in meeting Kathy Warren, and it's my pleasure to have done so. Because of this, I wish to include her poem in this book. Thank you, Kathy!

IWO JIMA

Four miles long, two miles wide,

With nowhere to run, nowhere to hide,

On the sands of Iwo Jima our Marines did fight

For 36 days, from morning through night,

In the bloodiest battle, historians say,

Too many men with their lives did pay.

And the government may tally the money it cost,

But you can't put a price on the lives that were lost.

No price for the mothers whose son never comes home,

Or the widowed bride left all alone.

And the innocent children left with no dad

Are robbed of memories they should have had.

But their loved ones did not die in vain,

For in our hearts they will always remain.

And the men who survived so gallant and true,

With honor to all – raised the red, white and blue!

--Kathy Warren
Seymour, Indiana

Those in the second picture taken on Iwo Jima, the one that went on to become so famous:

Mike Strank who was killed. I didn't know him very well because he ate his meals in another galley. He was a Sergeant and the oldest of the group raising the flag (about 22 years old). He was hard to get to know.

Franklin Sousley who was killed. He had a Kentucky twang and people mocked him. He had red hair and a temper to match. When not mad, he was fun to watch in the chow line. He loved home-cooked food and we gave him plenty!

Harlon Block who was killed. He trained as a Navy parachutist. He had a Texas drawl and loved to eat. He was so polite in asking for more meat... and he always got it!

Rene Gagnon. Of the six in the picture, he was despised by all of us. He was good-looking and wanted to make sure everyone knew it. He never fit into society. He tried several jobs in civilian life and died at 54 years old in 1979.

Ira Hayes. Our favorite one, a big Indian man was more at home taking a back seat instead of pushing himself to the front. He very seldom smiled, but you knew he was your friend. He was a wizard at cards!

John Bradley. Actually in the Navy, all of us respected him and called him "Doc." He would come through the line either in Navy uniform or Marine Corps'. Later he became owner of his own mortuary and died in 1994 at the age of 70. His son, James Bradley, wrote "Flags of Our Fathers" which was later made into a movie.

The last part of this book is being devoted to the following men (and patriots) who have been a part of my life. They are patriots because they were ready and willing to give their last full measure, their life, for America.

The first one is Francis Eberkamp from Jasper, Indiana, who was a Navy Corpsman in my Division on Iwo Jima. If there is anyone who deserves a salute, it would be a Corpsman in combat. They are out there in front, without protection, trying to save a man's life, under terrific fire from the enemy. Frances, I salute you!

The second veteran is James Lee Hutchison from the 8th Air Force in Germany. To know him is a complete pleasure. He has written two books, "Through These Eyes" and "Bombs Away," and is co-host of a local Veterans' Oral History TV program which tells it as it was. Thank you, Jim for being a part of my life.

The third veteran is Louis Hallett, who served America for over 22 years in Korea as well as Vietnam. I mentioned the Hallett family in the first chapter of this book. Louie and I grew up about 1 ½ miles apart, even though he was a few years younger than I. To be a part of Louis' life is an honor for me. We still meet at Walmart about two times a week and he is a joy to be around. Louis has received many awards for his years of service, including the Bronze Star, Purple Heart, Korean War Medal, Presidential Unit Citation, Distinguished Unit Citation, Korean Presidential Unit Citation, the Vietnam Presidential Unit Action Award, and many other commendations. He is and has been the Chaplain at our American Legion Post in Seymour for many years. He is the kind of person who would be willing to give his very life to save yours. Thank you, Louis Hallett, for what you are!

These few words were uttered by him and appear on the preface page of this book. For posterity I will end this book with the same conversation.

Not long ago, on a very cold and miserable evening in the dead of winter in Seymour, Indiana, I was sitting at Walmart where my wife, Jackie, and I were visiting with Louis.

I asked him, "Louie, would you go through another Korea and Vietnam in your life?"

He looked at me and said, "In a heartbeat!"

I peered back at him and asked why.

With tears streaming down the ruddy lines in his face   he said, "Because I love America."

In those four words, he captured and reflected the sentiments of so many of us, military and civilians,

"Because we love America."

--Frank Walker

Iwo
Jima
Today

THE FINAL INSPECTION

The Marine stood and faced God,
Which must always come to pass.
He hoped his shoes were shining,
Just as brightly as his brass.
"Step forward now, Marine,
How shall I deal with you?
Have you always turned the other cheek?
To My Church have you been true?"
The soldier squared his shoulders and said,
"No, Lord, I guess I ain't.
Because those of us who carry guns,
Can't always be a saint.

I've had to work most Sundays,
And at times my talk was tough.
And sometimes I've been violent,
Because the world is awfully rough.

But, I never took a penny,
That wasn't mine to keep...
Though I worked a lot of overtime,
When the bills got just too steep.

And I never passed a cry for help,
Though at times I shook with fear.
And sometimes, God, forgive me,
I've wept unmanly tears.

(continued on next page)

147

I know I don't deserve a place,
Among the people here.
They never wanted me around,
Except to calm their fears.

If you've a place for me here, Lord,
It needn't be so grand.
I never expected or had too much,
But if you don't, I'll understand.

There was a silence all around the throne,
Where the saints had often trod.
As the Marine waited quietly,
For the judgment of his God.

"Step forward now, you Marine,
You've borne your burdens well.
Walk peacefully on Heaven's streets,
You've done your time in Hell."

---*Author Unknown*

IN FLANDERS FIELDS

In Flanders fields the poppies blow
Between the crosses, row on row
That mark our place; and in the sky
The larks, still bravely singing, fly
Scarce heard amid the guns below.

We are the Dead. Short days ago
We lived, felt dawn, saw sunset glow,
Loved and were loved, and now we lie
In Flanders fields.

Take up our quarrel with the foe:
To you from failing hands we throw
The torch; be yours to hold it high.
If ye break faith with us who die
We shall not sleep, though poppies grow
In Flanders fields.

--Written by John McCrae, a Canadian physician who fought in WWI, and died of pneumonia while on active duty. (1872-1918)

ABOUT THE AUTHOR

Marion Frank Walker was born July 9th, 1925, at North Salem, Indiana, and moved with his family to Seymour, Indiana, when he was six years old. After completing high school ahead of schedule, he enlisted in the U.S. Marine Corps when he was 17 years old. Boot Camp was at San Diego, California, and then on to Camp Pendleton in Oceanside. From there he was shipped to Camp Tarawa, Hawaii. Even though he was a cook, he received the same training as everyone else, plus more, since he also became a flamethrower operator. After many months of training, he and his comrades boarded the USS Missoula which transported them to the island of Iwo Jima. The events of that battle are well-known in our history. At 0630, he climbed down the Jacob's ladder onto the Higgins boat, and at 0900, they hit the beach. He was part of Headquarters Company, 2nd Battalion, 28th Regiment, 5th Division, and their target was Mt. Suribachi on the green zone. He survived the entire 36 days of the bloodbath so aptly dubbed, "Hell on Earth." The survivors of that gruesome battle left the island on March 26th, 1945, having landed on February 19th, 1945, leaving behind nearly 7,000 comrades who had been killed. Finally it was over, and then it was back to Hawaii to re-form and go into Japan. He was on the high seas when the atomic bombs were dropped and then became a part of the occupation force at Fukuoka, Japan. After spending nine months in Japan, he was finally discharged in the fall of 1946, at 21 years old, having seen and experienced far more than any human being should ever have to endure.

LaVergne, TN USA
23 October 2009
161770LV00004B/7/P

"Let our object be for our country, our whole country,

and nothing but our country.

And, by the blessing of God,

may our country itself become a vast and splendid monument,

not of oppression and terror,

but of wisdom,

of peace,

and of liberty,

upon which the world may gaze

with admiration

forever."

DANIEL WEBSTER
1782-1852